# Prolog

The story begins with a teenage boy traveling with his family back to their home in Jackson, Mississippi from Arkansas. The time era is just prior to the Civil War. His thoughts are not in the politics or sectional conflicts of the day, he wants to go to Texas and become a cowboy and a ranger. He has visions of accumulating the free or dirt cheap grazing land to build a herd from the wild cattle and Spanish horses grazing on the open range. He is weighing this against the prospect of leaving his family and possibly never seeing them again. It is a ***"what if"*** that can change his life forever.

# Table of Contents

| Chapter | | Page |
|---|---|---|

| Chapter | | Page |
|---|---|---|

THe teenager was riding his four year old filly named "Charlie", completely oblivious to his present surroundings, lost in his day dreams. His favorite fantasy consisted of going to Texas and homesteading the free land. A man could homestead acreage and gather up all the free livestock including longhorn cattle and Mexican ponies roaming free on the open range. The young man's name was James Jefferson Walker, better known as James or just Jim. He was big for his age, approximately six feet in height with hazel eyes full of wonderment and his black hair closely cropped. He was riding his horse "Charlie" along what was called a road; however, it was just a wide trail leading back from Arkansas to his hometown of Jackson, Mississippi. He was with his family which included his uncle and among others his cousin, Billy Roy. His cousin, next to Charlie, was his best friend and had been since early childhood.

The family had been living in Arkansas for the past two years since his father was in the lumber business and had moved to the area for business purposes. They were going home to Mississippi much to the dismay of James. He had, for as long as he could remember, dreamed of moving to the frontier of Texas and becoming a Texas Ranger or at the very least a Texas cowboy.

The wagon train consisted of three wagons loaded with the furniture and personal belongings of the two families. Typically, It was the responsibility of James and his cousin to scout ahead to select the roads, river crossings and generally act as trail blazers. This enabled the two boys to have a lot of time alone. They discussed many things with "going to Texas" at the top of their list. The boys, who were barely sixteen years of age at the time, became excited just talking about it.

They had heard about Stephen Austin and the first colonies, the Texas Revolution with Sam Houston; Texas' time as an independent nation and its entry into the United States as a state in 1846. It was not uncommon to go to a neighbor's home and see it boarded up with a sign on the front door stating GTT or "Gone to Texas." It was an exciting time and took up much of Jim's thoughts and conversation between him and his cousin, Billy Roy. He would try again or as many times as necessary to convince his father they should go to the Texas frontier and grab as much of the free land as possible. Vast herds of cattle and horses from the Spanish occupation were roaming the vast prairies and were there for the taking.

The boys had made a pact that they would again attempt to convince their parents to go to Texas and if they did not agree they would, in the middle of the night, saddle their horses and ride off to the frontier alone. The excitement was difficult to contain and made the drudgery of the trail more bearable. As they reached Northeast Louisiana, the boys decided they would make one last attempt to persuade their fathers, but if this attempt was not successful they would saddle their horses and ride off in the middle of the night for the "Promised Land."

Later, Jim asked his father if he could talk to him about some very important issues. When he brought up the subject again, his father told him he was not going to Texas and that was the end of the subject. Jim told his father he would stay with him, working the new land until it was productive or as long as he was needed if he would go. His father again refused and said he did not want to hear any more about it.

Jim called on Billy and told him what his father had said. Billy stated that his father was just as adamant about not going. Jim said he was going if he had to go alone. They came up with a plan to saddle their horses and ride off while everyone was asleep the following night. The next day they filled their saddle bags with food and what they imagined they would need to get to Texas. Each boy had a shotgun and cap and ball pistol which was also crowded into their blankets and saddle bags.

Sometime around midnight, the boys crept over to their horses while asking each other just before mounting if this was really what they wanted to do. They both agreed it was as they silently rode their horses away from camp. A barking dog evidently woke the family and their fathers discovered their absence. They saddled their horses and took off in hot pursuit. The fathers overtook the boys when they boys came upon a plank fence. James and Billy rode their horses back so they could get a running start and jump the fence. Billy's horse could not clear the barrier, but James' horse "Charlie" was able to clear the top rail. As James and his horse landed on the opposite side, his father rode up. He attempted to jump the fence but his horse also was unable to do so. They sat on their horses and looked at each other across the fence without uttering a word. Tears came into their eyes as the possibility of not ever seeing each other again came into their minds. After what seemed like forever, James turned his horse west and rode off toward the promised land of Texas. The realization came over him he would probably never see his family again!

# 2

## The Journey to Texas

Of course, he did not know he would not see his family again, but in any event, he was so excited to finally begin his adventure of going to Texas. He knew enough of geography to know he only had one major waterway to navigate, the Sabine River separating the state of Louisiana from the state of Texas.

When he left his father's wagon train, he took only those things that were his property with the exception of some black powder and balls for his weapons. His horse (Charlie) was raised from a colt and was not only his private property but also his best friend. He talked to Charlie just as if she was a human and James thought sometimes she really could understand simply conversation. She did understand commands and followed them without hesitation. Spurs were not necessary and would be considered immoral to be used on Charlie. The slightest touch of the reins against the side of the neck would result with a turn in the desired direction.  He could mount from either side or a running mount from the rear with James putting both hands on the horse's rump and vaulting onto her back.

The love and closeness between the two became even greater as they crossed the new territory of Louisiana.  The route across the state is the approximate area of what is known today as Shreveport.  This was somewhat scary as James was alone and in a strange new world which he knew little or nothing about.  But it was a price he was willing to pay to achieve his dream.

The year was 1860 with the war drums being beat in both the northern and southern tiers of the country.  He had just turned sixteen and had more pressing and exciting concerns at the present time.  He had encountered a wagon train just west of Shreveport with the wagon master informing him of a ferry spanning the Sabine River.  He invited James to follow them and they would direct him to the crossing.  This not only provided direction, but also safety.  The Indians were almost non-existent in these territories;

however, there were still many outlaws and highwaymen who preyed on lonely travelers.

James enjoyed the many friendships he made while on the train, but he had also gained much useful information about Texas from the Wagon Master, who had made many trips to the state of Texas. After crossing the river into his new country he veered southwest down through the pine forest of East Texas toward Fort Parker. He marveled at the beautiful country, the magnificent pine forests and the rolling prairies with lush grass waist high. Every type of creature and game was abundant. They had not been around men enough to fear them.

The longhorn cattle and wild horses were everywhere, just waiting to be claimed and branded. James did not have the wherewithal to start a ranch, including the land or the money for supplies so he needed a job for a grub stake. The wagon master told him of a ranch just outside of Mexia that might be hiring. Mexia was a small town approximately two hundred miles southwest of where he entered Texas on the ferry. He decided that he would give the ranch a try but first he wanted to see the fort where Cynthia Ann Parker was captured when the fort was stormed by the Comanche Indians and a number of her relatives were killed.

Cynthia Ann lived with the tribe, married Chief Nocona and bore him two sons. One of these sons became the all powerful Chief of the Comanche, Quanah Parker. Quanah terrorized Texas until he was defeated in the Battle of Palo Duro in the Texas Panhandle. He was the last powerful Indian force in Texas. After viewing the fort, James rode over to Mexia to seek employment. He stopped at the general store and asked about any ranchers in the area who might be hiring cow punchers. He was told the Spillar Ranch just outside of town was owned by a recent immigrant from Illinois who had started a spread and was hiring cowboys.

# 3

## Becoming a Cowboy

James thanked the storekeeper and using the directions in a strange territory, eventually made his way to the Spillar Ranch. Reluctantly, he walked up the pathway to the main house and knocked on the front door. He had never applied for employment before and wasn't sure how to do it. But he needed money. So when Mrs. Spiller came to the door and introduced herself, he was quite impressed by her mannerism and physical beauty. She was considered to be an older lady, probably at least thirty-five years of age. Her hair was blond and flowed off her shoulders down her back almost to her waist. She had a turned up nose with radiant blue eyes, a beautiful lady.

James mumbled he was looking for work as a ranch hand. She said she did not do the hiring, but her husband, who was out rounding up strays, would be in toward sundown. She asked if he was hungry and he answered with a hesitating nod of his head. She provided a wash basin for him to clean up and fed him a hearty meal of stew and cornbread. This was the first good meal he'd eaten since leaving their home in Arkansas. Mrs. Spiller directed him to the woodpile at the rear of the main house and a chopping axe, explaining they never had enough kindling. He spent the rest of the afternoon chopping and splitting kindling wood.

Late in the afternoon, about dark, Mr. Spillar, with a few of his hands arrived back at the ranch. By this time, James had a sizeable stack of wood chopped and ready for the cook stove, fireplace and the stove in the bunkhouse. He heard someone calling his name, and he looked up at a large man, over six feet in height with ruggedly handsome features and a kindly expression on his face.

"I'm Mr. Spillar," the man said, "and I understand you're looking for a job on the ranch."

"Yes Sir", James replied sheepishly.

"How old are you, son?" Mr. Spillar asked. Where are you from?"

"I'm eighteen," James replied, stretching the truth a little, figuring that otherwise he would not get hired. "I came from Mississippi," he said, remembering that question.

"You think you have the age and maturity to handle the job?" Mr. Spillar asked with a twinkle in his eye. "It's a man-sized job, son."

"I think so, sir," James answered.

"Well then James, put your belongings in the bunkhouse and find yourself a bed," Mr. Spillar said. "I'll give you an opportunity for a few days to see if you can hack it."

James never looked back and within a few months was a top hand. He had a string of mounts furnished by Mr. Spillar. However, Charlie was still his number one horse and friend and would remain so as long as Charlie was alive. He developed friendships with the Spillar family that would last forever.

The most difficult part of the cowboy job was roping off a horse. Although he had been riding horseback all his life he had not been around a ranch environment i.e., riding fence, doing roundups, branding and roping cattle to doctor them. The foreman, Tom Green, took James under his wing and taught him what he needed to know in a gradual way. Before long he was the one of the best cowhands on the ranch.

# 4

## Raids and becoming a Ranger

One afternoon, Mr. Spillar called a meeting of all the cowhands in the big meeting room in the main house. Mr. Spillar mentioned the strong possibility of a raid conducted by a band of Mexican bandits. They had a hacienda they used as their headquarters and way station near Victoria when driving their stolen cattle and horses to Mexico. According to an informant riding with the bandits, they should arrive at the ranch at roughly midnight of that very night. He asked for anyone who did not feel right about defending the ranch to stand up. No one stood up. He also asked about viability of their firearms. Most were armed with cap and ball revolvers with a few also sporting break open shotguns.

The plans laid out by Mr. Spillar were to guard the herds by lying back in the scrub oak trees so as not to be seen until the bandits were committed. Because of James' age and inexperience, he was to be kept close to Tom Green, the ranch foreman. James was nervous and a little bit scared as he had not ever experienced anything of this sort. He guessed this was a small taste of what it would be like being a Texas Ranger. He would be tested to determine if he had what it takes. Yes, he was a little bit more than nervous.

Before they went out to guard the livestock, a steak supper with mashed potatoes and cream gravy was furnished to all the ranch hands in the big room with Mrs. Spiller in charge. This was probably even better than the Sunday dinners with Momma Walker's fried chicken. Mrs. Spillar said the blessing and asked the Lord to look after and protect her husband and boys.

After dinner, the cowboys rode out to the big pasture where the cattle were grazing. There were no fences except pole fences used for corrals primarily around the barns. These corrals were utilized for catching your riding horse by running the horse herd into the pen and roping your mount for the day. With no fences the horse and cattle herds could range far from the ranch headquarters. To maintain some degree of control, the herds would be fed in certain areas. They would not stray far from these areas where they were fed and of course, they had the Spillar Brand.

Mr. Spillar and Tom Green, as mentioned earlier, the ranch foreman and sometimes Texas Ranger, who was very experienced at disrupting bandit's lives, were in charge of the surprise party. The cattle and horses were grazing in a large meadow of lush grass with feed troughs. The pasture had scrub oak trees about half way up the side of the slight hills surrounding the meadow. Tom Green told James "come on, go with me." Tom took roughly half the cowhands and went to the other side of the meadow with Mr. Spillar taking the other half to the opposite side of the large pasture.

Now it was simply time to wait. Waiting was hard for James as he didn't know how he would perform. Tom rode up to him and seemingly sensing his anxieties stated he would do fine. Just stay close to him and don't try to do too much.

James thought of home and what he would be doing if his horse had not been able to jump the high fence on that distant night. He checked his guns, more from nervousness than anything else.

The moon was what could be termed a Comanche Moon or a full moon with nighttime visibility relatively good. However, the trees cast a shadow which could be deceiving causing an inexperienced Ranger to see things that may not be there. He saw movement along the edge of the trees was certain it was the bandits. He nudged Tom and pointed at the moving shadows but he quickly saw it for what it was, a buck deer and his doe.

It was a chilly November night and uncomfortable just sitting in the saddle. Along about midnight a large group of riders came in from the southwest and split up into two groups with one headed cautiously toward the herd of cattle with the other moving towards the grazing horses. The strategy, as explained to James while sitting on his horse and freezing, was to let the bandits trail off with their herds as if they had gotten away with their thievery, then hit them from both sides with all they had.

The bandits were seemingly very good at grouping up the animals and heading them back toward Victoria. After a couple of miles Mr. Spillar fired his rifle into the air which was a prearranged signal to attack. Tom told the boys to get after the rustlers with the horse herd and Spillar will attack the ones with the cattle. Before James knew what was happening, he was pursuing the rustlers and firing his guns. He had to be careful as reloading with a cap and ball weapon, on the back of Charlie, was a tough or impossible chore.

James was not sure if he hit anyone or not. They fired into the group and several fell out of their saddles. Because of the surprise, no one was seriously injured from their group. One horse was shot and had to be destroyed later at the ranch. Mr. Spillar's group had the same type of good fortune with only one rider slightly wounded and one broken arm from a horse falling with its rider into a ditch. The bandits lost five killed and eight to ten wounded. Mr. Spillar allowed them to carry off their dead and wounded but without his cattle and horses.

James was impressed with the professionalism exhibited during the skirmish.

"Tom, I was so scared I wanted to run before the encounter." James told the foreman.

"We were all a little afraid, but doing the job with that fear is the mark of a brave man." Tom replied.

This saying stayed with James and had a dramatic impact on his life; James thought to himself, *I thought I was the only one terrified. I'm not that much different from the rest of the cowhands.* For the first time he finally felt he was a member of the group.

He rode back to the ranch feeling good about their accomplishments, but a little sad when he realized he might have caused the death of another human being. This was something he had to get used to if he was going to ask Tom to assist him in becoming a Texas Ranger.

# 5

## The Tehuacana Battle

Tom and James were branding cattle the next week when out of the blue James got a surprise.

Tom told James, "You handled yourself pretty good during the Mexican Raid last week. We were wondering if you would like to do a scout with a few rangers over near Tehuacana. There has been some Indian activity in the area with three farmers slain last week."

James was both floored and pleasantly surprised by his invitation.

"We were thinking about riding over tomorrow morning if they can finish with the branding this afternoon. Mr. Spillar can't go with us but he agrees that something has to be done." Tom continued.

James didn't sleep much that night after putting Charlie in the corral and curried and grain fed. James did not ride Charlie every day as the rigors of ranch life are really difficult on a cow pony.  He had a string of mustangs furnished by the ranch that he used for everyday work.  But when he had something that needed dependability he always called on Charlie.

He stayed up late that night cleaning and oiling his weapons, two cap and ball revolvers and a double barrel break open shotgun.  James had been hearing about a new pistol manufactured by Samuel Colt which fired six bullets but did not require loading the powder and projectile separately.  It was an all in one cartridge.  Sam Colt was said to have made it based on the design of Ben McCulloch, the top Texas Ranger at the time.  You could load it on Sunday and shoot it all week. James thought *I'll have a gun like that when I become a full-time Texas Ranger.*  The statement was made using **when** not *if* as James had gained lots of confidence after the conflict with the Mexican Raiders.

Early the next morning they rode out of the corral heading in a northwesterly direction toward the small settlement of Tehuacana.  There were five from the ranch and they picked up another six on the edge of Mexia.  The number of Indians to be confronted varied, depending on whom you talked to and the number ranged from ten to thirty braves.  The thing that concerned Tom was why would they remain in that area for such an extended period of time?  As they rode out of Mexia, Tom stressed "Be exceeding careful as something does not seem right."  Usually, the Indians raided and ran but, this time they were seemingly in no hurry to leave.  There had been three deaths they knew of and possibly more by that time.

The community was approximately ten miles from Mexia with terrain consisting of lush grass with clusters of cottonwood and oak trees.  The trees were thick enough to conceal several men until you were upon them.  Tom's instructions to be exceedingly careful were foremost in his mind.

"Hold up, I've got something to say." Tom called out to the group once they were about five miles out of Mexia. The men reined up around the ranger.

"I'm still anxious about these Redskins and what they are doing for so long in the settlement. I think we should send a couple of rangers ahead to scout out the area, any volunteers?" Tom asked.

Without thinking, James volunteered. Tom was hesitant to accept him as a scout because of his age and lack of experience.

"Next time Jim." Tom answered.

Bill Smith and Jake McCord volunteered and were readily accepted. They were instructed to "hightail" it back and report as soon as any contact or sighting was made.

Jake McCord was one of the rangers joining the scout just outside of Mexia. He was, comparably speaking, an older gentleman and according to Tom, was one of the lucky few that had escaped the carnage inflicted on the four hundred Texians at Goliad and he had been with Sam Houston at the Battle at San Jacinto. He was asked to accompany Bill Smith to reconnoiter the area in front of the main force. He readily agreed.

The scouts positioned themselves in the tree lines on opposite sides of the prairie, roughly one-half to three-quarters of a mile in front of the main body of rangers. The distance varied depending on the topography. They kept within the tree lines to conceal themselves from the Indians. James could follow the scouts because he pretty much knew where they were.

Along about noon the scouts came back with an astonishing report. They had snuck in from the north and entered the small community unnoticed. The local citizens had been locked within the church. There were seven or eight wagons loaded with guns, ammunition, black powder, military weapons and supplies located within the Village Square. After they had reconnoitered the area as carefully as was deemed practical, Jake whispered to Bill Smith, his fellow scout, that they had better get back and relay this information to Tom Green. On their first few miles from the settlement, the scouts moved slowly, with caution, to avoid detection. When they reasoned they had enough distance between them they used their spurs to quickly get back to the main body of men.

When they rode up to the main body of rangers, Jake and Bill hurriedly sought out Tom Green and told him what they had discovered.

"There appears to be a group of Indians, probably around thirty and a Comancheros wagon train." Jake excitedly told Tom.

"I have never known of the Comancheros to be this far East. They stay pretty close to the Llano Estacado on the high plains of West Texas." Tom answered.

"I agree, but that's what it appears to be." Jake stated.

Tom called for a cold camp with sentries posted. He then held a meeting to inform the men what lay ahead. The men gathered around and listened intently to Tom's plan. Tom counted heads with eleven men present with the two rangers who had just returned from their reconnaissance. The ranger captain spoke with conviction and said, "Men, they have what looks like a force of up to thirty Comanche braves and a Comancheros wagon train." It appears the wagons are loaded with munitions and they ain't looking to hold a Sunday School Pray Meeting." Jake spoke up and asked if it could it be Northern Agitators stirring up and arming Northern Sympathizers?

Most of local people were well aware of the war clouds gathering over the nation, but that was in the Northeast, not in Texas. Tom told the men to not discount that possibility but it really didn't matter whether it was Comancheros, Northern Agitators or some other type of menace, they had to protect their settlements and their citizens.

"I want you to go back to the ranch and get as many of the ranch hands as possible." Tom told James after calling him off to one side. "Explain to Mr. Spillar the gravity of the situation and the need for more guns. My plan is to attack from head- on with flanking attacks from each side. To do this we have to have more men."

"I plan to attack early tomorrow morning after what I hope is a night of heavy drinking and celebration." Tom continued.

"It appeared whiskey was plentiful from what they could see." Jake said.

James rode hard back to Mexia and the ranch. Mrs. Spillar met him at the door and James asked if he could talk to Mr. Spillar? She said he was at the barn and James could find him there. Mr.

Spillar was talking to a couple of ranch hands when he rode up. James explained the situation and he understood the gravity of the situation immediately.

"How many men did Tom need?" Mr. Spillar wanted to know.

"He told me ten, but from what I understood about the numbers they would be facing, they would still be outnumbered." James replied.

In barely an hour, there were twelve men, including Mr. Spillar, with saddled horses and armed to the teeth. Mr. Spiller said goodbye to his wife and told her he would in all likelihood see her the next afternoon. He kissed her on the forehead, mounted his horse and they rode off toward Tehuacana. James thought to himself, *I'm getting to be an old hand at this Rangering business*. But he was a little jittery and he wondered if he was the only one that was a little nervous.

When they got back to the cold camp later that afternoon, Tom brought Mr. Spillar up to date on the situation. He seemed to be pleased to share the burden of command with the big boss. Most of the men had a pretty good idea of what was being played out. They spent the rest of the afternoon cleaning their weapons, making sure they had plenty of ammunition, playing cards and mumble peg. Most of these rangers were just kids who had grown up quickly, maybe too quickly. They were still children in years lived, but each had to grow up before his time, committing gruesome deeds necessary to perform as frontier rangers.

The night was dark with the clouds covering the moon. No fires were permitted due to the possibility of warning the outlaws. James had no idea how much sleep the other men got, but he got very little. It was cold but not unbearable. He wondered what his family was doing back in Mississippi and would he ever see them again. He finally dozed off seemingly about the time Tom shook him and told him to be ready to ride. The attack force was leaving in about twenty minutes. James had left his saddle on Charlie but the cinch straps were loose and the bridle's bits were unsnapped, hanging on the outside of her mouth to keep from grating her mouth. Charlie would stand over James while he slept, with the bridle reins usually on his chest or in close proximity. If something disturbing occurred the horse would nudge James until he was awake.

# 6

## The Attack

They Hurriedly checked their weapons, mounted their horses and waited for their orders. Tom divided the group into three fractions with him in charge of the frontal attack force and Jake and Mr. Spillar commanding the flanking groups.

The men were very surprised there were no pickets (enemy guards posted) on the outskirts of the camp. The force was divided up approximately one mile from the settlement with the two flanking movements angling off to each side. Tom would attack the larger force with a frontal assault. Due to the fact that no pickets were posted, the forces were able to station themselves in close proximity to the foe. The signal to attack was again, as it was with attacking the rustlers, a shot fired by Tom.

The shot was fired and the attack began just as the sun was coming up in the east. Even though the rangers were ready, it was a surprise when the shots were fired. They rode swiftly to the center of the settlement picking their targets as they went. The Indians were disoriented and as hoped, suffering from a case of drinking too much the night before. Several were killed and the rest ran away on their horses. Some attempted to surrender, but died in the attempt. The rangers were not overly sympathetic after suffering years of atrocities on the frontier.

The Comancheros were all captured and turned out to be natives of New York. Their mission was, as speculated earlier, to agitate and arm anyone who was an enemy of the South. They were blue bellied Yankees. Their wagon loads of munitions were seized and taken back to Mexia for storage. What to do with the Yankees was a dilemma. The general consensus among the Rangers was to shoot them. They were considered to be traitors or spies and in most cases they ordinarily would be condemned to the firing squads. Tom took them back to Mexia and turned them over to the sheriff who placed them in the local jail.

The local citizens were released from their confinement in the church with much gratitude demonstrated. No one was injured by the Indians or their Comancheros friends from the North. By 10:00 A.M., the situation had come under control with Mr. Spillar and Tom gathering up his rangers and appointing the local constable to organize the local citizens and dispose of the dead after the rangers left.

The town folks agreed to dispose of the Indian bodies by burning their corpses in a big bon fire, but only after scalping each one. The rangers had suffered no injuries due largely to the complete surprise and the tactics of the attack. The strategy utilized, i.e., the front assault with synchronized attacks on the flanks, would be made famous by General Nathan Bedford Forest in the coming War Between the States.

The group of rangers rode back to Mexia with a feeling that was not of joy but of having done something that was necessary to maintain safety and well being for the people on the frontier. The prisoners had been interrogated and they readily admitted that a civil war was a foregone conclusion and they were here to create mayhem in the midst of what they considered enemy territory.

James and his cousin Billy Roy had heard rumblings about the war but did not pay a lot of attention to it. These guys were cowboys and rangers and did not pay a lot of attention to political news or hardly ever read a newspaper. This, however, brought the problem to their attention. James heard the next week that the 10$^{th}$ Texas Infantry was recruiting a company over in Fairfield, a settlement about twenty miles to the east. He and some of the boys thought they would ride over and see what this was all about.

James was not quite seventeen at the time and his family nor for that matter, anyone they knew, owns a slave. It was just the idea that someone from "up North" could dictate how the people in the South should live. At any rate, the war would probably be over before they ever saw action. It was felt that one southern "country boy" would be able to whip ten northern city boys in a fair fight. Of course, as James and his southern friends would determine within a relatively short period of time, fighting the industrialized north would not be fair. And, the northern boys were not soft and made excellent soldiers. But they were young and they had proven themselves fighting outlaws and Indians. They wanted to go off on the great adventure and fight for their country.

# 7

# Going to War

Monday morning James and six other young cowboys rode over to Fairfield to see what the recruiter had to say about the 10$^{th}$ Texas. The person attempting to enlist the new recruits was the town mayor, a Mr. Routh. He was appointed as a Lt. Colonel of Volunteers. He promised adventure and glory to all who signed up. But they were going to train hard and go right into battle. They were going to leave Fairfield by the end of the week.

Almost all the guys in the units were from the local ranches and personally knew each other. A lot of these boys were brothers, cousins or had known each other for a long time. Everyone was concerned that the war would be over before they could get there. James told Colonel Routh that he had to go back to the Spillar Ranch to wind up some business, but he would be back before the end of the week.

James trip back to Mexia was a mixture of sadness and excitement.   He was sad about leaving the ranch where he had made so many friends and parting from a family that had been so good to him.  He considered Mr. and Mrs. Spillar as being surrogate parents and loved them dearly. But he was excited about becoming a member of the Confederate Military.

He arrived back in Fairfield and explained to Mr. and Mrs. Spillar how much they meant to him, but he felt it was his patriotic duty to join the army and fight for his country.  The Spillars were saddened but they understood.  James arrived back at Fairfield and reported straight away to Colonel Routh.  The Colonel immediately administered the oath and just like that, he was Private James Jefferson Walker.  He was assigned to a rifle squad as a rifleman.  His weapon was a 0.58 caliber musket that had a bayonet fixture on the end.   The first weeks were spent learning military drills and more drills.  James was not sure there was anyone present who really had a background in the military.

The Mayor was not a professional solider but, he had spent some time in the Mexican War and the Rangers. He seemed to know what he was doing, but they couldn't know for sure as they had no experience in these areas. They left the Fairfield area on Saturday morning and went to a region set aside in the East Texas piney woods near St. Augustine for additional training. The troops stayed there for approximately six weeks with the new troopers arriving every day. Each trooper was issued Confederate uniforms, rifles and all accruements necessary to go to war. They were also issued one half of a pup tent whereas two soldiers would have to partner up to have a complete shelter or tent. A great deal of time was spent marching and performing other types of military drills. They figured that if marching would win a war, they would be undefeated.

The recruits spent a lot time speculating about when they were going to move and where they would be going. One of the boys from Centerville was bitten one night by a coral snake. There was little anyone could do. By the time they discovered the incident, the venom was too far advanced to save his life. It was sad to see a young man in the flower of his youth, dying in front of you and having no power to save him. They buried him the next morning with the Unit's Chaplain conducting the funeral. It was the first of countless deaths they were to encounter over the next few years. The lucky ones would be buried with Christian words read over them; however most would be left in the open to the elements. These boys had no idea what lay ahead. Notwithstanding, the new troopers were getting antsy, they were ready to meet the enemy.

James became reunited with a boy whom he had worked with on the Spillar Ranch. They became close since they had joined the unit together and had been assigned to the same rifle squad. His name was Robert Johnson but they called him Bobby. He was eighteen and had been born in the West Columbia area about twenty miles west of Angleton. He was an outstanding cowboy, a good bronc rider and he could both read and write fluently. This was unusual for early Texas as the school systems were not that advanced with most kids home schooled if they were fortunate enough to have literate parents.

Bobby asked James one night as they were sitting around the campfire before taps if he thought he could kill someone he did not know. James told him he thought he had and related his experiences with the Mexican Bandits and the Indians at Tehuacana. He also stated he had never killed someone who was up close and personal. He added that he had always fired into a group with others firing at the same time, no one knew whose bullet had done the damage. James told him as far as he was concerned, that was good. Bobby replied that killing someone you don't know and is there simply because he is directed to be there did bother him. James thought to himself *Bobby is a very mature and seemingly has a lot of wisdom for his age.*

They woke up the next morning, which was a Sunday, and attended a church service conducted by the Chaplain who was a Catholic Priest. James had been raised in the Baptist Church but he felt that organized religion had little to do with one's relationship with God. James' concept of religion was that God should be exalted and his fellow man should be treated with respect and dignity. If you didn't follow those tenants you had a hard time, in his eyes, of being a Christian. It really didn't matter to what denomination the minister was certified, he was simply there to worship and glorify the Lord.

After the service and they had lunch, Colonel Routh called a meeting of the troopers in the 10th Texas to be held at the parade ground. The Colonel stated they had been at this site for six weeks and it probably seemed to them to be much longer. He said he hoped they had absorbed enough of the tactics to give us a fighting chance. He added, for them to pack their equipment, they would be moving out after first formation the following morning. The unit gave out an enthusiastic cheer as everyone was anxious to be leaving encampment. That evening, before dark, James and Bobby went by the freshly covered grave of the boy from Centerville. It was a sad occasion.

# 8

# On the March

After reveille and breakfast the next morning, they strapped on their packs, placed their muskets on their shoulders and marched out of camp to their next destination. They marched east toward the Sabine River which was the boundary between Texas and Louisiana. The trip across the river was done by ferry. The exorbitant charge for crossing the river caused them to believe the ferry operator was more gracious to the Yankees than he was to their forces.

They encamped again for a couple of days with rumors rampant. They were going to Virginia to join General Robert E. Lee, they were joining General Joseph E. Johnson in Georgia and lastly and as they would learn soon the correct one; they were going to march northeast through Louisiana and join Albert Sidney Johnson and his interdiction of the North's General Grant and General Buell at a place on the Tennessee River Called Pittsburg Landing or as the South called it, "Shiloh."

The unit left camp and marched from the small hamlet of Nacogdoches, Texas to Mansfield, Louisiana to Monroe, Louisiana and crossed the big Mississippi River at Vicksburg. The Southern people on the way treated them like heroes, but Vicksburg was the most patriotic city. It was difficult going through the city with all the temptations, e.g., food, drink, pretty girls, etc. rearing their heads at every street corner. Little did they know the 10th would be in a life and death struggle here in the greater Vicksburg area in the not too distant future?

After finally leaving the city behind them they headed for the settlement of Starkville and on to Corinth, Mississippi where they would join up with General Albert Sidney Johnston and march with him on to meet General Grant at Pittsburg Landing in Tennessee.

After a week of hard marching, the troops entered Corinth, Mississippi and were startled by what greeted them. It seemed all the buildings in the town, including private residences, had been transformed into hospitals. It appeared as if they had missed the battle. Bobby asked a Corporal

Jones of the 1st Mississippi what had happened. He replied that they had met Grant at Shiloh Church just over the state line in Tennessee on April 6th and whipped the army pretty good, but they did not follow up and at dark of the first day the Southern Generals allowed their troops to encamp with the complete victory to be completed the next day.

Corporal Jones continued, saying that during the night, General Buell arrived and disembarked with ten thousand Yankee troops which enabled Grant's forces to rout the Confederates the second day. And, the South lost one of the best, if not the best, generals on either side, General Johnston. This occurred in the Battle of the Hornet's Nest.

Corporal Jones tale of woe continued, stating the Southern Army recognizing it was hopeless, gathered its forces and headed back South toward Corinth. It had started to rain with the wagons creating big ruts in the road and the wounded crying out in agony and pain. The whole Confederate Army of the West would have been lost except for Colonel Bedford Forest who fought a rear guard action against General Sherman of "March across Georgia" fame.

General Forest was severely wounded during this action at the small hamlet of Monterey, but he did enable the defeated army to make it back to Corinth, Mississippi to regroup and to fight again. Some things became clear to James and his fellow troopers, the war would not be a short one and the glory would not outshine the true horrors of the conflict.

These mutilated kids were close to James' age, featuring horrific wounds to their bodies. The glory was quickly recognized as superficial and patriotism was taking a back seat to common sense. These kid soldiers with shattered bodies didn't own a plantation or slaves or other accruements of the landed gentry. He remembered what Tom had said before he left for Fairfield to join the military "It's a rich man's war and a poor man's fight." He thought to himself, *Life is just not fair.* One of the things that James was beginning to be aware of was necessary for "growing up" was to recognize the fact that life was not always fair.

The 10<sup>th</sup> Texas stayed at Corinth for about a month helping to fortify the area for Grant's attack which everyone knew was just a matter of time. But the large scale assault expected never materialized. At the end of the month they were ordered to pack-up and be ready to march again on quick notice. Where? No one seemed to know.

When the orders came to march, they were headed south toward what each thought was the road to Vicksburg. The rumors were widespread they would be reinforcing General Pemberton's Command at Vicksburg which was regarded by the Confederates as the "Gibraltar of the West." It was commanded by, as stated above, General Pemberton with approximately 33,000 troopers with some navy men sprinkled within that number. They marched south by southwest going through Oxford (site of the University of Mississippi) and instead of continuing their southward course they turned almost due west. They crossed the Tallahatchie River by boat and marched west again through the Mississippi Delta until they came to mouth of the Arkansas River where it emptied into the Mississippi River.

The 10$^{th}$ Texas again crossed by boat to the Arkansas side and set up their tents until all the units were across. James and Bobby gathered wood for a campfire and cooked their rations completely unaware what their next move would be. The platoon Sergeant called them together and told them to set up their tents; they would spend the night there. Tomorrow, he told them, they would be marching to Fort Hineman or its older and more accepted name was Arkansas Post." The stronghold was named after Confederate General Thomas C. Hindman of Arkansas. The location had been constructed on a bluff 25 feet above the north side of the river and forty-five miles downriver from Pine Bluff. The unit would fortify the Arkansas River against northern incursions against the cities of Pine Bluff and Little Rock.

# 9

## Arkansas Post

It was manned after the arrival of the 10th Texas with roughly 5,500 men, primarily Texas Calvary, dismounted and redeployed as infantry. The force consisted of three brigades under the command of Brigadier General Thomas J. Churchill. By the winter of 1862-63, disease and their position at the end of shaky supply chain had left the garrison in a poor state. The base also served as a base for disrupting shipping on the Mississippi River and provided support for Vicksburg.

The sergeant told the platoon to get a good night's sleep and be ready to move out after reveille the next morning. James and Bobby just looked at each other in some degree of bewilderment and crawled into their sleeping bags.

The next morning the 10th Texas moved out on the northern side of the Arkansas River through country that was completely new to the troopers.

This country was strange to these country boys and to some degree was treated as a new adventure to them all. James was not a much traveled man, but he seemingly was much more traveled than anyone else in his unit. The sun was sinking in the west when they saw the salient of Arkansas Post. They camped for the night on the outside of the fort; they could, and would, become permanent residents tomorrow.

The time period following their arrival at the fort to the time of the battle was spent in building ramparts; primarily gun emplacement and rifle pits. There was a lot of boredom and rumors primarily about the Yankee's movement against Vicksburg. A lot of time was spent digging rifle pits which provided a view of the river for approximately one mile in both directions. There were posted sentinels but the troopers themselves also kept a keen eye peeled for possible enemy forces moving up or down the river. James and Bobby were expecting company in the form of blue clad troopers coming from the East at any time.

James missed his best friend, Charlie. The 10$^{th}$ was a Texas Calvary Unit; however, they were being used or deployed as a dismounted or infantry unit. James had been forced to leave him at the ranch in Mexia. It was good, probably because it would have been difficult to feed him. Food was scarce for the troopers with seemingly none or very little for the animals. The grass for the animals was almost non-existent during the fall and winter months.

The lack of adequate supplies on a weak supply line contributed to malnutrition. This resulted in severe cases of childhood diseases, along with the inadequate nutrition, proving to be a deadly combination. Several of the fellow troopers in James' unit succumbed during their encampment at Arkansas Post. It was a sad state of affairs that the young men away from home for the first time died without family nearby to comfort them. And, James missed Charlie. He really missed Charlie. The winter was hard with much ice and snow, but the protection provided by the fort's living quarters proved to be adequate.

After a month of boredom, James and Bobby were sitting on the ramparts when they saw several large boats approaching from the east. They sat on the wooden planks and stared, they finally realized the boats meant they were being invaded by the Northern troops. James and Bobby ran to the supply hut and were issued as much shot and powder as they could carry and lodged themselves in one of the rifle pits nearby. The feelings turned from absolute boredom to excitement and maybe a little bit fearful. Bobby commented to James "man, there are a lot of blue troopers on those boats."

There were a lot of enemy in the force coming up the river. Union Major General John A. McClernand, a politician who had secured a military appointment from President Lincoln had arrived with an army sized offensive consisting of approximately 33,000 soldiers and sailors. McClernand was short on military training but was long on political ambition. He had deceitfully gained his military force for an offensive against Vicksburg. He called his 33,000 man force, the Army of the Mississippi and without the permission or knowledge of either President

Lincoln or the overall commander at Vicksburg, General Grant; he launched the offensive against Arkansas Port hoping for glory and ensuing political gain. He also ordered Grant's right hand man, Major General Sherman to join his forces as his second in command without Grant's permission.

On January 9$^{th}$, the force started up river toward the fort with Sherman corps overrunning the Confederate trenches. Bobby and James retreated behind the protective wall of the fort. The Navy under Flag Officer David Porter, on January 10$^{th}$, moved his gunboats towards the fort and opened a bombardment. James and Bobby peered out from the slits in the rifle pits as the fleet sailed past the fort effectively cutting off any thought of retreat or resupply. The shelling from the ironclads and the Yankee artillery on the south side of the river in point of fact suppressed the fort's big guns. This envelopment caused General Churchill to turn over his sword to McClernand that afternoon despite the orders to defend the fort at all costs.

The casualties were relatively light if you were not one of them. Of the 5,500 Confederates at the fort, 4,791 surrendered. A number of the rebels in the outer perimeter of the defensive line simply climbed out of their rifle pits, walked into the woods and escaped. James and Bobby and most of their unit were not so lucky. Their rifle pit was on the interior of the defensive line and they had nowhere to go. They had no choice but to throw down their muskets and surrender.

"I've never surrendered before and it's scary, shameful and disgraceful or at least that's the way I feel." Bobby told James with tears rolling down his cheeks.

A Yankee three stripper (buck sergeant) arrived and addressed their unit.

"Take all your military accruements and put it in a pile in front of your ranks. Keep your canteens and shelter halves. After you have piled your equipment as directed, just sit down in place until they know where you'll be going." The buck sergeant announced.

"Where will we be going?" one of the fellows asked.

"I don't know for sure, but I expect some of the troopers would be going to Camp Douglas in Chicago and some would end up in Camp Chase in Columbus, Ohio, "the sergeant answered.

They were fed about the middle of the afternoon. It was the first decent meal they had in months. They even had seconds if they wanted them and everyone did.

The prisoners were issued blankets since this was January and it was cold at night. They got up at 6:00 the next morning and were fed a hardy breakfast.

Bobby asked James "why do you think all those steam ships or paddle wheelers are lined up in the river?"

"That is probably our transportation to our new residence in Chicago or Columbus." James replied with a look of resignation and despondency on his face "It is so hard to accept our surrender; I think I'd rather have died fighting."

Shortly thereafter, they were called to attention and placed in columns of deuces (twos) and marched down to the landing wharf. They were marched onto the paddle wheelers to begin their journey to the prison camps. James and Bobby had the good fortune to be placed on the same boat. However, it was very crowded; finding your own space to eat and sleep was a nightmare.

Of course, James did not know that the Yankees suffered a total of 1,047 casualties, killed and wounded. The Confederates suffered almost their entire force as casualties who constituted their total contingent, almost all by surrender, except the ones who slipped away before and during their capitulation. It constituted one of the largest surrenders of Confederate troops west of the Mississippi River prior to the end of the conflict in 1865.

James, with his friends and fellow soldiers sat on board their ship all that day and into the night. They finally got started about two hours after the sun had finally dipped below the small hills to the west. Rumors were rampant on where their final destination might be. They were even gambling on at which prison camp they would finally end up. The Yankees didn't seem to mind as they were using confederate currency. The money was worth nothing in the north and not much more in the south. Approximately two hours after they had started, they came to the mouth of Arkansas River where it empties into the Mississippi River. The boat turn north, but that did not solve the mystery of their final destination, Camp Douglas in Chicago or Camp Chase in Columbus, Ohio.

# 10

## The Escape

James nudged Bobby the first morning on the big river and asked him "Do you notice anything?"

Bobby with a puzzled look on his face said "What am I looking for?"

"See how close the boat comes to the shore from time to time?" James replied.

"I haven't been paying much attention." Bobby answered.

He told Bobby "I hope the guards haven't been paying much attention either." It looked like an ideal way to escape. As an afterthought he asks Bobby "Can you swim?"

"Yes, I can." Bobby replied.

James told Bobby "I've noticed the ship will come near the shore from time to time and if we could work our way, without causing suspicion, to the edge of the boat, we might have a chance to jump overboard and swim to shore."

James and Bobby spent the rest of the day maneuvering to the outside railing. About four or five in the afternoon there was a lot of shouting with rifle fire coming from the mid-section of the ship. Evidently, some of the others had the same idea as James and Bobby and had jumped overboard in a group.

It was carnage as the guards shot the prisoners as their heads bobbled in the water, attempting to swim to shore.

Bobby, with a look of terror on his face, said to James "I'm just glad we didn't try that, it was simply suicide."

"Not so fast, I think it can be done. Have you noticed the trees and other debris floating down the river, especially near the shore? We could time our escape by jumping into the water and use those trees to shield our bodies from the rifle fire. The ship is traveling north going against the river's current, while the trees are being swept downstream by the current. If we can jump behind one of those logs and keep low we can in a short period of time be beyond rifle range." James explained.

61

Another consideration was the farther they traveled north on the river the greater distance they would have to spend in hostile territory. About dark, with the sun settling in the West, the ship veered toward the western bank of the river to avoid a sandbar. Bobby and James noticed there were a lot of tree stumps and limbless trees as if they are coming from a logging operation.

Bobby said "I don't really want to do this but if we are this is probably the best opportunity we will get."

"I agree, let's go!" James said.

Each boy placed their hands on the railing and vaulted over into the Mississippi, hoping to hit nothing but water upon their landing. They hurriedly ducked under the water and came up behind a large floating log. It seemed all the guards were shooting and the boys were concerned about the log coming apart. After about ten minutes the distance made the marksmanship difficult from their boat, but then they noticed several bullets coming in from behind them. It was rifle fire coming from one of the boats to their rear. They had to shift their positions to avoid the bullets incoming from the rear.

After the ships got past the sandbar, they steered out into the middle of the river leaving them to their devices. After dark, they paddled their tree, which had saved their lives, to a small inlet or slough where they could wade onto the river bank. They were wet and cold. This was the middle of January and it was starting to rain.

They stayed in a protective cove on the river bank to shelter them from the rain and wind. They snuggled with each other, unashamed, as their main concern was warmth. Surprisingly, both of the troopers slept until they were awakened by a rooster crowing from apparently a nearby farm. They had no idea where they were except somewhere on the western bank of the Mississippi River. James estimated they were in Northern Arkansas or Southern Missouri.

"If we are lucky we will be in an area which is sympathetic to the Southern Cause. There are some real bad people in parts of Missouri that have no love for us or the Southern Cause." He said.

63

When they got up the next morning and looked at each other, it wasn't pretty. Their clothes were still wet and muddy. They had not shaved or conducted any personal hygiene since the morning the fort capitulated and not much for the two days prior to that. They were not hungry but they would be getting that way in a relatively short period of time. The key now was to determine where they were and how to get home without being shot.

James and Bobby knew their military unit did not exist anymore. It was completely destroyed at Arkansas Post with no one to report to. James' thoughts were to get back to Mexia and reorganize. Bobby, who was from West Columbia, Texas, about two hundred miles southeast of Mexia had ridden up with some of his friends when they heard the Spillar Ranch was hiring and they were in need of jobs.

"What I want to do?" Bobby almost shouted "is to go home."

James reminded him that they could be in enemy country and to hold his voice down. Bobby said he got so excited about going home he forgot where he was and could not help from almost shouting. Despite the fact that they were dirty, hungry and for all practical purposes lost, they were euphoric to be alive and free.

James knew the Mississippi ran north and south and the boat was going north and he knew they were on the west side of the river so they pretty much knew which way to go to reach friendly territory. They had seen some semblance of smoke off in the distance so they knew a settlement of some sort was near. They just didn't know what it was or if it was friendly or not. They also had to be careful because they could be mistaken for deserters and shot without an opportunity to explain.

There were a lot of confederate troops becoming disheartened and saddened with the war and they simply went home. Most of the troops in the ranks owned no slaves or a plantation to protect. The war theme they went to war singing was a conflict that could be over before they arrived on the field of battle. The epigram most often quoted after years of privations and seeing your friends slaughtered, hardened the innocent young men hearts and they determined rightly or wrongly it *was "a rich man's war and a poor man's fight."*

James looked over at Bobby, "let's go over to the settlement and see if we can talk to someone who might be willing to help us."

The settlement was about two miles west of the river. After about a mile they came upon a relatively well-maintained ranch/dairy farm with a large herd of Holstein cattle and several horses.

James asked Bobby "Do you think we should approach these people or go into the village?"

I think we probably will have better luck with the country folks than city persons." Bobby answered.

"I agree" said James as he walked up to an older man coming out of the milking barn.

"Good morning, Sir" said James to the man who looked them over carefully. James said "we are Confederate troopers who escaped from a steam ship taking us, we think, to a prisoner of war camp in Chicago." "We were captured at Fort

Hindman or Arkansas Post a few days ago. We don't know exactly where we are and if this is confederate or northern territory. We are, or were, with the Tenth Texas Dismounted Calvary out of Fairfield, Texas. We are trying to get back to Texas and home." James looked the man square in the eye and said "We are putting our lives in your hands without knowing where your loyalties lie."

The man said "my name is Thomas Weatherby, with my loyalties being with neither side. We have tried to remain neutral and so far we've been pretty fortunate. Some of the neighboring farms and small settlements have been attacked by the likes of Cantrell or Bloody Bill Anderson's bands of cutthroats. We've been left pretty much alone by the Missouri Red legs and the Kansas Jayhawkers."

"The Yankees and the Confederates have been so busy with Vicksburg that we don't see much of either side. It appears to me what you really need is a bath, clean clothes and a meal. We will worry about getting you back to Texas after these necessities are taken care of," Mr. Weatherby told the weary young men.

He said he had a couple of boys about their age and his main concern was keeping them out of this horrible war. James and Bobby could not believe their good fortune and followed Mr. Weatherby like two puppy dogs to the barn and the stock watering trough. The container was about three feet high and about ten feet across. He told them to take off their clothes and crawl into the trough.

He said, "Don't worry, there are no girls here at the barn and while you are taking a bath I will see if I can find some decent clothes for you to wear. I think my son's clothes will fit ya'll as you appear to be about their size."

They bathed and even played some in the water. The excitement of being free and happening onto Mr. Weatherby was mind-boggling. James and Bobby had a long way to go to get back to Texas, but a big hurdle had been cleared or so it seemed. Mr. Weatherby soon appeared with clothes and even with socks. They had not had socks since the ones they wore from the Spillar Ranch. The clothes were somewhat loose, but that was due to James and Bobby's lack of nourishing food over the past year, but they felt really good.

Mr. Weatherby took them to the main house and introduced them to his family, including his three daughters and two sons whose clothes they were wearing. They never asked if the boys were twins, but they appeared to be about the same age and looked a lot alike. Mr. Weatherby evidently had explained their plight since everyone was being so nice to them. They were seated along a long table with the center filled with wonderful food in bowls; large platters of hot cornbread and biscuits, rolls complete with butter and big glasses of iced tea or sweet milk, whatever your preference. After dinner there were different types of pies, it was wonderful. The boys had never had a meal this good ever, even at home or the Spillar Ranch.

Mr. Weatherby suggested they stay for a few days at the farm to rest up, gather their strength and figure out their route and method of getting home. He said there were facilities in the barn's tact room for them to stay. He added that it might look suspicious to visitors coming to the farm to see two strange *trooper aged* boys. The barn was a step up from what they were used to in the army. They had an outdoor privy near the building with comfortable beds in the tact room itself. Bobby told James he bet, based on the facilities there in the barn; they weren't the first soldiers in trouble the Weatherbys had helped. The barn and those areas in proximity has a distinctive smell of cow manure which was fine as both Bobby and James were farm boys who were used to the odor. It kinda reminded each boy of home. It is difficult to explain to city people how the smell tends to make country boys feel comfortable.

# 11

## The Guerrilla Attack

*The* first few days spent at the farm consisted mostly of eating and sleeping. They would help on the farm anyway they could when there was no one around. They had to be careful as there were people in the area who had differing loyalties and would attempt to collect bounties or rewards for turning in deserters. On the third day at the farm, Mr. Weatherby called a meeting of the family with the local sheriff present. The sheriff stated they had captured a member of the Bloody Bill Anderson militia and while being interrogated had said they were planning a raid in this vicinity to secure riding mounts and cattle for slaughter. Also, they would kill anyone at the facility. They were just a bloodthirsty bunch. The sheriff thought it was going to the Weatherby Farm.

The sheriff said "We are not sure of the date or time but we feel it would either be tonight or tomorrow night." The sheriff continued, "We will move all the civilians, like the women and children to other safer locations as soon as possible. I will place my militia in the various buildings to give Mr. Anderson and company a warm welcome. So, let's get to it, we don't have a lot of time."

Mr. Weatherby said to Bobby and James, "This is not your fight, you don't have to stay, and you can leave now."

James looked at Bobby, who gave him a nod of his head and said "No Sir, your fight is our fight, but we will need some guns. We lost our weapons at the surrender."

The next few hours were spent moving out the family and any other non-combatants and preparing the home for a siege. The farm house was large and well-built to sustain the Midwest winters and spring storms. It had wooden window shutters with slots or openings ideal for firing a rifle. By five o'clock in the afternoon they were as ready as they were going to be. Mrs. Weatherby and her girls fixed a meal for all before they left for safety. After the posse had taken up their defensive positions, all they could do was wait.

The men in the assemblage were very similar to the ones James was familiar with back in Mexia. These were men who led their lives in an ordinary fashion but came together for common security. When danger threatens, they assembled as a unit for common protection. That was also the genesis of the Texas Rangers.

Bobby and James took positions in the barn with several of the other fellows. They were friendly but no one really asked personal questions, which was good. Most the group were local, i.e., farmers, merchants with a couple of school teachers, etc. They had some time together early in the evening but most of it had been spent discussing the probable struggle before them.

James and Bobby had never heard of Bloody Bill Anderson and did not know what to expect. They were told he considered himself a military arm of the confederate army but in reality he was a bloodthirsty cutthroat who followed no rules of warfare. The confederate army wanted nothing to do with Bloody Bill. He was a cold bloodied killer who did not discriminate between gender and the age of his victims.

Several member of the group played poker and a number played dominos to pass the time. However, sentries were posted around the perimeter of the farm to give adequate warning of the adversary's approach. The boys went out onto the porch and they marveled on what a beautiful night it was. The moon was full with good visibility. It reminded James of nights back in Texas and what they called a Comanche Moon. The Comanche came down across the Red River from Fort Sill in the Oklahoma Territory into Texas to make their raids while the moon was full and they had good visibility.

James was looking towards the small settlement when Bobby tapped him on the shoulder and said "What is that movement on the prairie to the southwest?"

At that point, one of the sentries came riding hard up to the house shouting "They are coming!"

Mr. Weatherby shouted "Take your places men; it appears that our guests of honor are arriving."

Mr. Weatherby had issued Remington repeating rifles which were new to the boys, but were astonishing. Seemingly, one man could hold off an attack of several by himself. They found a position in a window of the main house where they had a wide field of fire.

The group of riders was getting pretty close when one of the men inside the house shouted "that's Anderson's group, that's him out in front."

Mr. Weatherby shouted "let them have it, boys" and the entire farm erupted with shot and shell. The first fusillade emptied many saddles and also several horses suffered gunshot wounds. It appeared that Anderson was wounded but, he stayed in the saddle and rode away. At first count, it appeared about half of the attacking force was killed with several more wounded but were able to escape.

A number of the men grabbed their horse's reins and were attempting to mount, but they were restrained from giving chase by Mr. Weatherby.

He said "they're beat, let them go off and lick their wounds, they won't be attacking anyone for a long time, if ever."

After the battle, there were several saddled horses wandering around the farm house and barn. The unwelcome, dead intruders were loaded in the back of a horse drawn farm wagon and taken somewhere on the back of the farm for burial in a mass grave. Mr. Weatherby told the men to run the horses into the corral and shut the gate. He called Bobby and James over and told them to pick out a couple for themselves. Riding those horses will beat walking back to Texas.

The horses were high bred with excellent saddles and bridles outfitted for men who made a living in the saddle. Bobby picked a blazed face sorrel and James singled out an appaloosa, which was a rare but an excellent breed. Mr. Weatherby told them to check out their mounts and see if everything was useable. He told them they could stay there as long as they desired, but he understood if they wanted to get back to Texas and home.  He asked them to at least stay the night, eat a good meal and leave the next day.  He would help them map out a route and furnish them with supplies for their journey.

He also let them keep a rifle and an abundance of ammunition taken from the fallen gunmen.  To travel hundreds of miles through what could be hostile territory without a weapon was almost suicidal.  It felt good to have a weapon, if not for anything else; it could be used for obtaining food.

# 12

## The Journey Home

The journey home was tentatively mapped out going through Little Rock, Shreveport, with a southward push from Dallas to Mexia. After a good night's sleep and hearty breakfast the boys rode southwest toward Little Rock. Their hearts were heavy leaving the Weatherbys, but the thought of going home was exhilarating. James was concerned about the thought of having a horse that might compete with Charlie, his horse at Mexia. Hopefully, Charlie was alright and well kept at the Spillar Ranch.

They rode near the towns to maintain direction, but mostly skirting the populated areas and even ranches were to be avoided. It would be difficult to explain why they were not members of an organized military unit. Also, since the surrender of Arkansas Post, federal gunboats and organized Yankee military units were ranging as far to the west as Pine Bluff and Little Rock. After the first day of dodging patrols and civilians, the boys decided they would travel only at night, at least until they crossed the Red River back into Texas.

About noon of the first day, they came across an abandoned shack with bunk beds and a cook stove. They were afraid to start a fire due to someone seeing the smoke and coming to investigate. It appears that the shack had not been used for some time so they felt relatively safe. There was also a pole corral where they could keep their horses. Due to the excitement of the previous day, sleep did come easily. As a result, both boys were asleep by the time they lay down on their crude beds.

When James awoke, Bobby was still sleeping peacefully. He shook him gently and he looked up and asked James what time it was. James told him the sun was a big orange ball in the west as it was just now setting. It was time they eat some food and start their trek to the Texas border. After a cold supper, they saddled their horses and rode in a southwesterly direction with the full moon helping to maintain their bearing. After riding almost the entire night they found a thicket of live oak trees where they could hide themselves and their horses. They each decided this would do nicely to maintain cover during the daylight hours. They were fortunate enough to find good water for themselves and grazing for their horses which they kept hobbled in a protected cove.

They were getting more excited as they neared the Texas border; however, they kept reminding themselves, they could not relax their diligence until they were home in Mexia. James kept reminding himself and Bobby they had to be attentive not only for Yankees and Confederate Militia who might think they were deserters, but this was 1863 in Texas without a protective military to guard the frontier against marauding Indians. The United States Calvary had been removed to fight in the War Between the States. Part of these troops went north to fight with the Yankees and part went to fight for the Confederacy, but they left no one to guard Texas from Indian attacks.

Even with the troops stationed on the frontier, you could count on a raid from the Comanches coming down from Fort Sill during the full moon each month. These raids would be concentrated on the outlying western counties such as Jack, Palo Pinto, Wise and Parker. The Indians prior to the Calvary leaving did not venture east of these counties due to the high probability of being cut off from their escape route. But with the military off fighting a war among themselves that was no longer a threat.

Most of these were not killing raids but were utilized for stealing stock, preferably good horses. The Indians were excellent judges of good horse flesh. They would also steal young children to nurture as their own or trade them back to the white eyes for a profit. Cynthia Ann Parker, who had been abducted during the raid on Fort Parker and was raised as a Comanche, married Chief Nocona and raised a family. She was re-captured and died of despondency because she could not go back to what she considered her people, the Comanche.

# 13

## The Indian Raids

On the second day after leaving the Weatherbys, they met a wagon train of six wagons coming straight at them. They started to veer off but Bobby said "let see where they are going in those ox pulled wagons."

There were two fellows riding hard toward Bobby and James. Bobby shouted "Who are you and where are you going?"

The boys were taken aback and as one man replied excitedly, "We are heading to far East Texas to avoid a large band of Indians who had jumped the reservation and was killing and plundering."

The two riders said they were from up in Denton County and they were running from a large band, estimated to be more than a thousand, of Indians thought to be primarily Comanche and Kiowa.

This was a killing raid with the farms, ranches and small settlements plundered with the women raped and one and all killed before moving on. A large group of settlers had forted up at Forts Richardson and Belknap, northwest of Weatherford and were surviving. It seemed the only people who did survive were the people who secured themselves in ranch houses with a large group of their neighbors. The Indians would bypass these strongholds to find easier pickings. It seemed that due to the lack of the military to protect the settlers, the Indians were moving more boldly, deeper into East Texas than ever before.

The men asked Bobby and James if they would like to go with the train until it was safer to travel.

James said "No, we will travel mostly at night with Mexia hopefully being south of the present path the Indians were traveling."

The men told the boys not to travel west or north but, to turn south as quickly as possible and travel at night as much as doable. One man asked how far it was to Mexia with James saying he was not absolutely sure but he figured about three hundred miles as the crow flies. The boys thanked the men, spurred their mounts and headed East with a little bit of fear in their being.

They rode hard until they reached the settlement of Corsicana just as the sun was coming up in the East. They were attempting to cross a creek or small stream when something caught James' eye. He whispered to Bobby to hold up until they could determine what the movement was. They moved their horses behind a thicket on the side of the creek and saw about five Indians riding down the middle of the stream. They were riding beautiful mounts and were armed with single shot Springfield rifles. It appeared from a distant they were young braves, probably on their first raid. Among the group was one older brave with a feathered headdress, suggestive of being some sort of chief. The chief had a ceremonial spear with what appeared to be scalps hanging from one end

The Indians appeared to be stealthy, like they were sneaking up on someone. Except for the noise made by their horses jostling through the creek water they made no noise. The boys cocked their repeating rifles, held their breath and said a small prayer that they would not be seen by the Redskins. This was not to be, as a mockingbird flew directly in front of James' horse causing him to jump sideways. The Indians were startled but recovered quickly. They brought their rifles up to their shoulders but James and Bobby fired first with their Remington Repeaters, creating death and confusion among the braves. The chief and the two front braves dropped immediately with the rear two turning quickly to make their escape, but they were shot within fifty feet of the first volley.

It was not a pretty sight. Five lives snuffed out with four appearing to be as young as they were. They had to make sure no one escaped to get help and come after them. They also knew they had to get as far away as possible. These braves would be missed and the main body would come looking for them. Bobby wanted to gather up the lances, especially the one of the chief but James said they had to get going and fast.

They spurred their horses and sprinted through a line of trees for concealment, heading in a southerly direction. After a couple of miles the pace was slowed to a lope and after another few miles the pace was slowed to a trot. The horses needed some rest and a trot provided somewhat of a breather. The horses had to be as fresh as possible in case they ran into the Indians and had to run. It was night, but the moon was still full with cover of some sort an absolute necessity. They had no idea how many Indians were in the main body and where they were.

They figured they were near the eastern edge of Dallas County and if they turned south and stayed on that course until morning they would end up somewhere around the settlement of Ennis. Several house fires were seen in the distance, but the boys did not check them out. They felt certain it was the Indians performing their shockingly cruel acts. The two of them were simply not enough manpower to offer effective help. The sun was coming up in the eastern horizon when they decided to stop. As best as they could figure, they were between the settlements of Ennis and Corsicana, almost home.

They found a clump of trees and bedded down with their horses hobbled nearby.  They slept the sleep of the innocent until about four in the afternoon when Bobby woke James and said "Let's chance it and start early."

James replied "No, not this close to home.  I would hate to get scalped when all they have to do it wait another three or four hours."

Bobby said "You're right, I'm just anxious." They continued to set in the midst of the thicket and talked about home, ever mindful of the Indian peril.

This was a January evening with the days getting dark between seven and seven-thirty and a chill in the air.  They un-hobbled their horses and saddled them a little after seven, mounted and headed in a southwestern direction.  They figured they were about fifty miles from the Spillar Ranch from their campsite.  They estimated their time of arrival at about three or four the following morning if no Indians were encountered.  This created exhilaration in each boy which was difficult to put in plain words.

They were anxious to get back home as they had been away for almost two years.

Bobby was from West Columbia, which was a substantial distant from Mexia, but they had talked about Bobby staying and taking his old job again at the ranch. James felt there was a need for more hands as so many had left to go to fight for the Confederacy.

# 14

## Coming Home

About two thirty, coming in from the north, they saw the small settlement of Tehuacana sitting on the high hill. They swung to the west to keep from attracting attention and rode hard on toward Mexia. Their excitement was growing as they were only a few miles from Mexia.

They rode directly down Main Street from Tehuacana into the settlement of Mexia. When they crossed over into the corporate limits of the town, they were surrounded by a crowd of gun toting men. At head of the group was Tom from the Spillar Ranch. He did not recognize James, but James recognized him.

He said, "Tom, it's me, James."

Tom yelled out to a man on the edge of the group "bring me that torch" and a big smile appeared on his face when he recognized James. He asked, "What are you doing back home I thought you were fighting the war against Northern Aggression."

James said, "I was captured at Arkansas Post and escaped a few days ago with my friend, Bobby You remember Robert Johnson; he was working at the ranch when we joined together." James asked Tom "What are you doing here at three in the morning?"

Tom answered, "A large group of Indians are on the prowl. By best estimate, over a thousand braves left the reservation at Fort Sill in the Indian Territory about a week ago on a killing raid. Supposedly, the leader of the group is Chief Santana, a wily old Indian who lost his son on a raid and he is out to settle some scores. They say he carries his son's bones in a sack on his horse. They also say he has the bones with him on this raid."

Bobby spoke up and said "We noticed many houses burning from a distance between Ennis and Tehuacana. Tom added those houses were probably vacant as most farmers and ranchers had been warned and had forted up in the nearest communities."

Tom stated "The Indians aren't stupid; they usually don't attack unless the odds are in their favor."

The number of the hostiles was again estimated to be over a thousand braves, but they would split up into smaller war parties with most groups numbering less than a hundred warriors. That was still a substantial number of combatants to contend with. The typical small settlements were hardly more than that number; however, most of these men were hardy individuals who could shoot straight and ride hard; on the other hand, they were hardly a match for the redskins whose main function in life was to hunt and to be a warrior.

Tom said, "We had warned all the settlers in the vicinity of Mexia to come in for their protection and to defend the town. And as far we know everyone had obeyed the appeal."

James asked Tom, "How long had this been going on, the forting up of the towns?"

Tom said, "This was the third night and so far it has been effective. No one has been lost or harmed in any way. We were just lucky we were warned in time to protect ourselves."

One of the other men spoke up and said "they weren't so lucky in the western settlements like Jacksboro, Palo Pinto, Decatur, Weatherford and Young County, they were hit hard." Of course, that was the frontier which the savages would come into contact with first on their murderous raids.

The military garrisons at Fort Richardson (Jacksboro) and Fort Belknap (Graham) had been garrisoned with militia but the real soldiers had gone to fight in the Civil War. That is not to say there were not some really good troopers which included, among others, the Texas Rangers. These men were at the forefront of any fight and included Charles Goodnight and his friend and business partner, Oliver Loving. These men were along with the civilians and Texas militia forted-up at Fort Belknap.

Goodnight had a ranch that was one of the first to be attacked and no one presently had any idea what its state of affairs might be. The Indians started at the confluence of Elm Creek and the

Brazos River in Young County. They followed it down into the interior of the state killing men, women and children living on the farms and ranches. Goodnight's Ranch was located on Elm Creek near where the Indians started their murderous rampage. The incursion would go down in history as the Elm Creek Raid. Even though it covered most of North Central and parts of East Texas, it was always known as the *Elm Creek Raid.*

The band of savages split-up east of Weatherford just west of Fort Worth. One group headed up through Denton County and on into East Texas while the other group went south of Fort Worth into the Ennis and Fairfield areas into what is known as Central Texas. With no organized military contingent, the only alternative for the Texians was to gather together for protection.

James asked Tom, "What is the state of affairs out at the ranch?"

Tom answered, "They've got about forty men boarded up in the bunkhouse and the main house. The horses are in the corrals and will be protected.   As you know, the horses are the first thing the Indians will go after."

James asked Tom, "What about Charlie, is she alright?"

"Oh yeah," Tom replied, but I think she never got over being left behind when you left."

James asked, "Is it possible to go to the ranch tonight?"

Tom said, "I think it would best to wait until the sun is high in the sky. The men are a little skittish and trigger happy due to the lack of sleep over the past few days. These men have had some really ghastly experiences during this period of time."

James told Tom and the rest of the men about their experience with the four braves and the chief.   As they explained the incident it made them both sad, but they had no alternative but to kill the Indians.

Tom stated "Don't be too hard on yourself, you had no choice, it is kill or be killed."

"I'm not certain what will happen if the siege doesn't end within the week. They are running short on food, but they have what I feel is a sufficient amount of ammunition. The men are getting edgy and they are concerned about their families."Tom continued.

Bobby asked "What are the alternatives?"

Tom said "Not many are open to us. If they don't get help within three or four days they will run out of food. They've been on short rations since they first arrived here. They need help in the form of a large military unit. Nothing less will force these savages back over the Red River into the Indian Territory."

Tom said "Most of the Mexia citizens and people from the surrounding area have barricaded themselves in the town center and waited for the main attack. So far, they had only been subject to small attacks seemingly to feel out their strength. They've killed three Indians and wounded several more, but the injured red skins were able to remain on their horses and get away." Chief Santana according to the information obtained was with this group.  But, nothing is certain with rumors running rampant.

One of the men in the group, who had arrived about midnight, stepped forward and said that General Sterling Price, with his regiment was over near the Louisiana Border.  The General apparently wasn't aware of the gravity of the situation when he was with the General yesterday morning.  If someone could ride to his headquarters and make him aware of the circumstances, he could kill or run what was left of the rascals back into the Territories.  Tom, who everyone looked to as the man in charge, said they could send someone on a fast horse to bring him to our rescue.

James spoke up quickly and said "I'll go!"

Bobby quickly said, "It would be more practical to send two separate riders to stand a better chance of at least one getting through."

Tom said, "That is a good idea and each man should take at least two extra horses. One horse can be ridden down relatively quickly in a pursuit." He added, "Someone has to get through and bring us help!"

"Tom, can I go by the ranch and pick up Charlie? She has always been more durable, smart and fast."

Tom replied "I think that would be a good idea, she is the corral near the big barn, the one with the tack room."

James said "thanks, Tom I appreciate it."

# 15

## Riding for the Calvary

There were about two or three hours of darkness until daylight when James arrived at the ranch. He had to be careful not be shot by mistake by the people at the ranch. He stopped roughly one hundred yards out and hollered who he was and he was coming in. A voice from the barn answered to come in but keep his hands away from his guns. After he got within a short distance James was recognized, resulting in a happy reunion. He explained his reason for being there, to pick up Charlie and ride for help from General Sterling Price. They found a lariat from the equipment room as well as his old saddle and bridle.

One of the ranch hands had caught Charlie, saddled her and brought her to James. It was another happy reunion with Charlie raring, nickering and moving her head up and down in a joyous way. James mounted Charlie and moved out from the ranch as quickly as possible, explaining he had to get as far away from the center of the Indian's concentration. His idea was to ride one horse and before he got so weary, he would change his saddle to the other horse to keep the two horses as fresh as possible. He had initially planned to take two extra horses until he realized he could use Charlie. Charlie was so durable and strong he felt comfortable with only one extra. And, the extra horse was the one he had acquired in Missouri and rode back to Mexia.

He left the ranch and headed east carefully skirting the settlement of Teague and riding somewhere between the small towns of Fairfield and Buffalo. He figured the Indians were encircling the communities waiting for an opportunity to strike. The live oak thickets could hide a party of braves until you were up to them.

It was scary but James had no choice and Charlie seemed to sense the danger. He rode hard until the first rays of the morning sun started to rise in the east. He wanted to get as far away from the concentration of the Indians as possible.

James, sensing that Charlie was getting a little weary leaned forward, put his open hand on Charlie's neck and lovingly rubbed it, gently letting her know his fondness for his friend. He guided them into a thicket of live oaks and changed his saddle from Charlie to his other mount. He kept up a good pace as he wanted to use the cover of darkness to get as far away from Mexia as possible. He was heading in the general direction of Nacogdoches, but again avoiding the towns. James had some close brushes with the savages but, they were in small groups and seemingly not willing to commit without overwhelming odds.

Due to the desperate state the people in the Indian ravaged areas were, James decided to continue after the sun was high in the sky. He had ridden briskly all day without taking a break for a noon meal. He had some jerky that Tom had given him to eat. He would take a bite from time to time. He would stop every two hours or so to rest the horses and change his mount. It was important to keep the horses fresh in case they ran into the savages.

About three in afternoon, some outriders were sighted in the far distance. It didn't appear to be Indians, but he was not close enough to be certain of their identity. They were apparently riding straight toward him so he pulled up behind some trees so he could see who they were before they seen him. When they got closer James could see the rider in front had a small flag which was the Stars and Bars, the Battle Flag of the Confederacy. James put the reins in his teeth and rode out with his hands pointed to the sky. You had to be careful because there were some very dangerous people in the area. A lot of the military would shoot first and sort it out later.

The troopers said they were scouts for General Sterling Price's Regiment. James informed them who he was and of his mission, which was to find the military and bring some relief to the beleaguered citizens of North and Central Texas. The man in charge was Lt. Leroy Vann who said that the regiment was approximately ten miles to the rear. He said General Price had outriders to the Northwest, the west and the southwest. He knew from people fleeing the havoc there was a problem, but the numbers and locations were yet to be ascertained.

James said "Lt. Van, the best estimate of Indians is one thousand braves." They are split up, but each group is sizeable and cannot be openly met on a field of battle with our scattered groups. They don't have the ammunition or manpower to defeat them. And, they're running dangerously low on food."

Lt. Van said it would take at least three hours to get a battalion up after James told him they were about ten miles to the rear.

Lt. Van added, "A battalion is roughly five hundred riders with the rest following within half a day. Large bodies of men take time to move."

It was roughly four in the afternoon and taking everything into consideration i.e., going back to the main body of troops, getting a battalion ready to march and arriving back where James and the outriders were, would probably take, as previously stated, about three hours. The march back to Mexia would take another fifteen hours with an estimated time of arrival of between eight or nine the next day. Whatever their time of arrival there would be a lot of appreciative citizens?

Lt. Van hand motioned to his two scouts, bringing them to the front of the small group. He told them "to ride back to the main body of troops and convey to the General that the Indians had been found and to bring the troops, post-haste."

"I'm sending both of you in case something happens to one, the other can continue the journey." He continued, "I cannot emphasize enough how important this is. The lives of countless men, women and children hang in the balance. We will wait here for you to return, so this young man (referring to James), can guide us to the besieged areas." With that the scouts saluted, spurred their mounts and headed east as quickly as their horses could carry them.

James spent the next three hours making Lt. Vann as well-informed as possible on the general geography of the area where they would probably be meeting the hostiles.  James explained it had been approximately two years since he had been a resident of the territory.  He had been fighting for the Confederacy and had just returned after escaping from the Blue Troopers on his trip to Camp Douglas in Chicago.  He had a good idea of the terrain and other important factors.  But Tom Green, the ranch foreman and sometime Texas Ranger, would be the most useful person to obtain critical information.

James asked Lt. Vann if the general would be receptive to other people's opinions."

Lt. Van told him they are not in a strict military environment here, "why don't we address each other by our first names, my name is Leroy and you can just call me Leroy."

Leroy said "Unlike most Field Grade Officers, General Price encourages input from other sources and considers it carefully when making his final decision."   After the discussion about the upcoming military encounter with the savages, the conversation became somewhat personal.

Lt. Van was born and raised in a small hamlet in Mississippi.  He had graduated from the University of Mississippi at Oxford with a major in architecture.  He said "I wanted to build things like structures, bridges, etc. and here I am, destroying

103

them." Leroy continued, "These creations are more than just things, they are the bringing together of something of substance into existence." He continued, "Something that can enhance man's existence on this earth." He caught himself and quickly added, "I know I sound like a nut, but I like to think I can leave something useful for mankind when I leave."

James said "No, I think everyone should feel as you do." James thought to himself that, *Leroy was different from the people he had known in the past.*

The conversation began to become more normal as Lt. Van asked James if he had family in the area.

James told him that he wasn't married and his folks were in Jackson, Mississippi. He had not seen them in almost four years. James in turn asked the Lieutenant if he had family and he replied that he did. He told James that he had married when he graduated from college and they had a son almost a year old. And, he had not seen his wife in over a year and he had never seen his son.

He was in mid-sentence when he stopped and said, "I think I hear the Battalion in the distance."

Sure enough, the large cavalry unit could be distinguished in the early evening twilight by their flags and military uniforms.

Lt. Van said "I guess we'd better go back to the military politeness of addressing me by my military rank, but I will always be Leroy to you."

As the troopers arrived, James could not help noticing the man in front with the large plume in his hat and the stars of a general on his uniform. He would find out later this was General Sterling Price in person.

The General rode up to Lt. Vann and asked him to bring him up to date. Lt. Vann introduced James to the General and explained he could be more helpful in terms of describing the terrain, estimating distances and number of hostiles. He explained to the General "James had worked on a ranch at Mexia before leaving for active duty with the 10th Texas. He had only been back since escaping from Arkansas Post where he had been held captive for a few days."

James said "the terrain consists of small hills, blue stem and similar prairie grass and most of the trees were post oak thickets. This will be the type of terrain they will encounter between here and Mexia and after they arrive there.

I would put out some outriders two or three miles in front for warnings and ride like the devil to get to Mexia. The souls there need you desperately. Ás far as the numbers, I only know there are a lot. I've heard numbers ranging over a thousand, but I feel that's an over estimate. I would guesstimate between five or six hundred.    You have to understand no one other than the savages themselves know for sure.    The ones we have encountered are Comanches with some Kiowas with them.  My time in Texas has made me aware that the Comanches are without a doubt the best light Calvary in the world, so don't take them lightly.    I've had some experience as a Texas Ranger and I know the Rangers regard the Comanche on horseback as a force to be reckoned with."

General Price told Lt. Vann, with his unit, to ride ahead of the main body and to get back to him if anything was discovered that was of concern.    Lt. Vann asked James to go with him with the General in agreement.  They turned their well-rested horses west and commenced a trot. They would stop every two hours to allow the horses to rest and the larger column to catch up. They would also leave colored pieces of cloth on the trail that the General's Scouts could follow.

James noticed numerous fires which were evidently burning ranches and farms so the devils had been busy since he passed the night before. James prayed the people who lived in these houses had made it to safety. Along about midnight, the moon came out from the clouds with good visibility. This was good and in some respect bad in that it improved their visibility, but it also enabled the Indians the ability to see them. After about four or five hours, they encountered a saddleback mountain or hill with maybe twenty braves on horseback looking down into the valley. James and the troopers were riding inside a line of trees making them difficult to see.

They were outnumbered, but James didn't think they were outgunned. They were equipped with repeating rifles while the redskins, as far as they knew, still had the old single shot, breech loading rifles. The repeating rifles made less, more.

Lt. Vann said "Let's take them; we can circle around to their rear and attack. We know where they are, but they don't know where we are. That was a huge advantage." They stayed in the trees until they were to the Indian's rear. They tied their horses to trees and climbed the hill on foot, being careful not to step on any dry limbs or twigs.

After gaining their position to their rear, they counted. There were actually eighteen Indians and they were all on horseback. That was enough to go around. They were not sure what they were doing, but it didn't matter. Lt. Vann, using economy of force, assigned each of the troopers' particular targets. This was to make sure that several of the men did not fire at the same Indian and allow others to escape to fire at them.

Most of the troopers, after the order to fire, were given responsibility for at least two Indians. Lt. Vann went quietly to each man after they were in position and pointed out their area of responsibility. He explained that when he dropped his arm, they were to begin firing. When the order was given, the troopers began firing and the Indians dropped off their horses with no discernible noise other than the rifle fire. James was impressed with Lt. Vann and his detail in the professional way the assault was enacted. They did not go to or inspect the fallen hostiles. They simply re-mounted their horses and rode west toward Mexia.

They stopped at a small settlement about twelve miles southeast of Mexia called Teague. They were greeted at first as unwelcomed as the Indians until they convinced the good citizens who they were and their mission.

James told Lt. Vann "I think it will be better if we stop here and ride in with the General and his troopers. We need to act as a buffer before the whole force descends on Tom and his force in Mexia."

"The troops should be getting here before long," added Lt. Vann. "It takes longer for a large body of men to move, but they lost a substantial amount of time having to take care of those hostiles on saddleback. They should be getting here soon." It was good policy to let the people in Teague know that a large body of troopers will be arriving. When it's dark and you hear a large herd of horses coming your way you would probably think it was Indians." "It can create a real dangerous situation."

# 16

## The Calvary Arrives In Mexia

A Texas Ranger was in charge of the citizens at Teague. He offered James and the troopers' fresh coffee which was very well received. They were on their second cup when they heard the rumble of many horses' hooves striking the soft sod surrounding the settlement. It was the Calvary riding hard, coming across the open prairie to the east. General Sterling Price with his plumed hat was in the forefront leading his Calvary to the rescue. James and Lt. Vann mounted their horses and rode out to greet the General. Lt. Van told the General "This is hostile territory, but heck; probably everything in this part of country is now occupied by Indians."

James said "I'm not telling the general how to conduct his military affairs, but I think it would be practical to leave a detachment here as these people are in great danger with hostiles everywhere. The rest of the battalion can go on to Mexia and wherever they are needed. I'm of the opinion that the Indians, when they see the Calvary in such force, will head back to the Indian Territory."

"They need to relieve the citizens in Mexia and the surrounding areas." General Price stated "I appreciated the advice from someone local and it seemed to be a sound idea."

The general left a detachment at Teague and with a forward wave of his hand moved to the Northwest toward Mexia. As they rode out of Teague, the town's people were cheering the soldiers to show their thanks. James was dead tired but the demonstration of gratitude seemed to put a little vigor into his body. He rode astride Charlie with a little bit of pride.

As they rode to Mexia, numerous hostiles were spotted, but they kept their distant and none offered any unfriendly initiatives. The force arrived at Mexia to the stressed cheers of its citizens.

Tom ran up to James and said "They are really glad you're here they were attacked last night and lost three men. If the Indians had sustained the assault they would have run out of ammunition. It would have been hand to hand with rifle barrels and hatchets. Thank God and you, James; the army made it just in time."

James asked Tom "Have you heard anything from Bobby?"

Tom answered "No, not a word."

James added, "I am worried as I saw many hostiles as I rode east to get the army."

Tom said "Bobby is probably still riding north of where you encountered General Price and his Army."

"I hope that is the situation." James replied.

The supply wagons with the ammunition and food came rolling in about thirty minutes behind the column. One wagon was left in Teague as all of these settlements were almost down to nothing. With sentries posted, the troops along with the citizens, settled down to a meal of army chow and were happy to get it. It was about noon with most of the soldiers dragging around from two days without sleep. The citizens of the settlement were in a bad state from the lack of sleep and food for almost a week.

James sacked out under one of the supply wagons and slept like a baby for about four hours when he awoke with someone shaking him.

He looked up and exclaimed "It's Bobby!"

"Yep, it's me. I didn't think I was going to make it for awhile. I know one thing, that horse I picked at the Weatherbys can run I encountered a group of probably ten Indians and they chased me for about five or so miles. It was my fault as I thought I was too far east for the redskins. I became sloppy and careless and almost paid with my life." James, Bobby added, those Indians are good horsemen and they ride good ponies."

James asked Bobby "Have you had anything to eat and I know you're dead tired, right?"

Bobby answered "Well, I'm hungry, but I don't know if I can keep my eyes open long enough to eat."

James took Bobby over to the supply wagon with the army cook rustling up a plate of food for him. He sat down in the shade of an oak tree and started to eat. He took a few bites and slumped over, fast asleep. James stretched him out and took a saddle blanket and placed under his head for a pillow. Bobby had a tough two days and had earned his rest.

About dark, a group of men rode up from the direction of Tehuacana and asked to see the man in charge.

Tom said "Well, I'm a Texas Ranger and I have been the person responsible until General Price arrived today. I think the civilian militia is my responsibility and the military is the General's. They do work together for the common good.

The man in charge of the new arrivals said "My name is Charles Goodnight and this is my friend and business associate, Oliver Loving." Mr. Goodnight said, "We have been riding hard from the Jacksboro and Weatherford area." They had been chasing a large war party over that distance. "They have an estimated five hundred braves surrounded in a box canyon about ten miles distance." Charlie added, "If they knew our number they wouldn't stay surrounded for long."

"They had heard General Price had arrived and they needed him and his troops to help with the problem." Mr. Goodnight stated, "The braves in that number were simply too large for the rangers and the citizens to handle. But if you hurried, you might get there before the Indians became aware of our weakness.

Tom was taken aback, he had heard of Charles Goodnight, but he had never actually met him until now.

James ran over and woke Bobby and exclaimed "They were going "Indian Hunting" with Charlie Goodnight and a group of Texas Rangers."

Bobby jumped up and said "you're joshing me, right?" James said "just saddle your horse and hurry or we will be left behind."

They had ridden for about an hour when Charlie Goodnight rode up to the two boys and Tom who was riding with them. He said "You people know this country better than any of us." He added, "The Redskins are only two or three miles to the northwest. We really need a strategy or we could get a lot of people killed. I think it would be a good idea to make a wide sweep around the area where the hostiles are located."

Tom heartily approved. James while making his encirclement noticed all their horses were tied to a rope line at the Northeast corner of their campsite.

As they arrived back at Mexia, Tom and Charlie were concerned about the casualties that would result from an assault on an entrenched enemy.

James was listening intently and then he spoke up "I know I'm just a private in the 10$^{th}$ Texas if it exists anymore, but I have an idea I'd like to offer."

General Price, Charlie Goodnight and Tom said "let hear it."

"As we circled their encampment, I noticed they had their horses at the northeast corner tied to rope lines." "If we could go in and run off their horse herd, the Indian threat would be over. An Indian without a horse is a beaten Indian."

The men, General Price, Charlie Goodnight, Tom and even Bobby all agreed that was an excellent idea. And, it should hold the casualties to a minimum.

The moon was still full with night visibility good, too good for the men who were going into battle. Everyone was saddled up and ready to shove off at seven with the attack tentatively set for 8:00 PM. The plan was for the majority of the men to feint an attack against the main body of the Indians while approximately a dozen men cut the rope lines the horses were attached to and take them far enough from the main body of the hostiles so they could not reach them on foot.

To ensure the Indians did not become a dangerous light cavalry again, the horses would be slaughtered. This was not a pleasant thought, but it was necessary to protect the frontier. It was a long walk back to the Indian Territory, but it would be a long time before another large attack like this one was made again. James and Bobby went with the ones who were to get the horses.

Half of the men snuck up and killed the few Indians who were guarding the remuda while the other half, including James and Bobby, cut the rope lines and herded the horses away from the Indian camp. It was over in just a few minutes with the Indians guarding the herd dead and the captured horses moving away from the encircling hostiles.

James thought to himself, *it was easy, too easy.* The number of troopers made holding the Indians quite easy. A number would attempt to break free but they were easily shot with no prisoners taken. The citizens, after a couple of weeks of siege, with their women raped and men, women and children killed and scalped, no quarter was given. The old axiom, "the only good Indian is a dead Indian" was certainly holding true in this part of Texas.

The next morning, Charles Goodnight with the approval of General Price and someone who could speak Comanche, held up a white bed sheet to gain a parley with the Indians. The old Chief, who started all this killing, walked out to meet Charlie. James could not hear what was said, but the chief was throwing up his hands and making loud noises. Charlie turned to walk off when the Chief motioned for him to return. The interpreter said later, the chief refused to yield and Charlie told him to go to hell. He said "He was going to kill all their horses and if he didn't agree, he would kill all the braves." He added "That's what he really preferred doing." He then turned and started to walk off when the old Indian called after him and agreed to his terms.

A mounted guard surrounded the Indians until morning when they were lined up and surrendered their weapons. Some of the young braves tried to break out with most being killed; however, a few made it. These few would steal horses from the ranches and farms in the area. These places of habitation were vacant as the residents had long since sought refuge in the settlements. A few of these people were caught unaware in the beginning but the word was spread and the farmers and ranchers came in droves to the settlements.

Charlie told the old chief to take his people and go home. He would ask General Price to send a detachment to follow them until they reached their sanctuary across the Red River at Fort Sill, Indian Territory. The old chief was mad, but he knew he had no choice. He gathered together his senior braves to work out the details and at 10:00 AM, he had them in columns to start their long march. He asked for their horses but General Price and Charlie Goodnight were unwavering about not allowing the Indians their mounts. The Indians with their horses, Charlie felt sure, would be raiding and killing again before they got to Hillsboro.

The General sent one hundred men with repeating rifles to trail these villains north with orders to give no quarter. The rest of the men went to their respective settlements and homes except for a selected few who would do the grizzly chore of killing the horses. The men who participated in the fight were given the opportunity to pick out two horses for their own personal use. Killing the horses was a very unpleasant task.

# 17

## Life Getting Back to Normal

Most of the farmers and ranchers in this region had adequate warning to seek safety in the towns. The buildings seen burning at night was vacant with their owners safely secured in the settlements. Their fate was substantially better than the residents of Parker, Palo Pinto and Jack Counties on the northwesterly frontier.  These were the first counties encountered by the rampaging hostiles on their natural path from their sanctuary in Indian Territory to Texas.

Charles Goodnight and Oliver Loving went back to Mexia to gather their extra horses and say goodbye to the town's people.  Oliver Loving was an older man who basically took charge of the logistics of running a military camp.  Charlie was a Texas Ranger who was a top hand (cowboy) and was an excellent Indian fighter on the frontier. When his folks came to Texas from Illinois, he rode all the way on a horse, bareback, at the age of nine.  After the soldiers left to fight in the Great War people like Goodnight, Loving and others had to form militia units just to survive. Goodnight and Loving also had become trailblazers who drove large cattle herds to New Mexico, Colorado and

Montana. But there were times when they had to take time off to protect their lives and property.

After the excitement was over, James and Bobby realize how tired and worn-out they were. They snuck off with a bedroll they had found somewhere and slept for about twelve hours. When they woke, they went directly to the Spillar Ranch and renewed friendships with people they had not seen for over two years. The first person James recognized was Mrs. Spillar, standing on the front porch of the main house. She saw James and Bobby and she came off the porch and started running toward the pair. When she reached the duo, she threw her arms around first one and then the other. She was crying and shouting for joy at the same time. It was good to be home.

She said "Mr. Spillar, after the General and the Army arrived, went out on the range to check on the livestock." The cows should be fine as the Indians actually hated cows since they felt they ate the grass that should be used as feed for their buffalos.

Sometimes they would maliciously kill the cows out on the range as an act of vengeance. This was characteristic of a killing raid, but it was out of character of a raid to steal horses. As they were catching up on the years of their absence, four or five riders were seen coming across the prairie to the southwest. Mrs. Spillar exclaimed! "That appears to be Mr. Spillar now!"

The men rode up into the yard where Mrs. Spillar and the boys were standing. Mr. Spillar did not know James and Bobby were back as he had not come into Mexia during the past three days. When James picked up Charlie at the ranch, it was dark and only a couple of the ranch hands were aware of his intentions. The ranch had been made into a strong point and Mr. Spillar stayed there to act as the commander in charge. Several riders from town had brought the news that the Indian Menace was over and he felt safe enough to check on his cattle.

Mr. Spillar was overjoyed that James and Bobby were back. He asked them how they were able to return when their military unit was still in the field. James explained "The 10th Texas was no more." He further explained, "The Tenth was killed or captured at Arkansas Post and for all practical purposes ceased to exist."

Bobby added, "We didn't know what to do so we came home." Bobby went on to explain their escape by jumping overboard from the Mississippi streamer transporting them to the prison camp, Camp Douglas in Chicago, Illinois.

Bobby asked about the livestock, If the Indians had killed a substantial amount of the herd?

Mr. Spillar said "No, we were really lucky the Military arrived in time. I think they thought they had time to do their killing later."

Bobby told Mr. Spillar "You owe a debt of gratitude to the Military, but also to James, who rode almost to the Louisiana Border to find General Sterling Price and bring him to Mexia."

James added quickly that "Bobby also went on a different route to accomplish the same purpose, it was fate that he happened on the Military and Bobby did not."

Mr. and Mrs. Spillar were simply overwhelmed with this knowledge. They had not seen these boys in over two years and they show up and save not only the ranch and Mexia, but the whole area from Fort Belknap in the northwestern part of the state to the pine forest of East Texas. The Spillars were very proud of the boys and Mrs. Spillar exclaimed they should be honored with a shindig to show their appreciation. Everyone in the area would be invited. The boys felt kind of taken aback by all the attention, but Bobby told James it would be an opportunity to see old friends and make new acquaintances.

# 18

## Gratitude to James & Bobby

James said to Bobby "We might even meet some girls; our love life has really suffered over the past two years."

Bobby asked in jest, "what is a love life?"

The boys were invited to supper in the main house and a good time was had by all. They were surprised that their beds in the bunkhouse were still as they had left them over two years ago. They got a good night's sleep, the best they had since leaving the ranch. They got up the next morning, ate breakfast, and saddled their riding horses and went to work on the ranch as if they had never left.

James could not believe the joy of being back in the saddle, herding the cattle and doing what used to be considered as mundane ranch chores. Just having enough food to eat, a bed to sleep in and not getting shot at, was almost overwhelming for the first few days. Sleeping on the ground, worrying about varmints, especially snakes, could and did made the soldiers' nervous and jumpy day in and day out. The boys did not know for sure what lay in their future.

James told Bobby "If they form a new unit we can join and go back and serve out the war, but I'm going to work here on the ranch until that day occurs."

Bobby told James "That sounds good to me."

The get together was to be a *"celebration that the Indian Menace was over"* and to honor James and Bobby. It was to be held on Saturday night in the new Mexia Community Center. This would be the first time the facility would be used and what a way to christen the new building. James and Bobby were excited as they were to be the guests of honor.

The week passed quickly and Saturday night and the celebration were upon them. Bobby and James had nothing to wear except their old confederate uniforms which were almost in sheds. The City of Mexia led by Mrs. Spillar, bought an assortment of clothes for each boy. Two pair of khakis and one pair of heavy work trousers, three work shirts and one dress shirt, a pair each of work and dress boots and an assortment of underwear, handkerchiefs and a hat to be selected of their own choosing.

When the boys took their baths in the horse tank and dressed up, they felt very special. Neither boy had ever had this much of a wardrobe in their whole lives and they knew who to thank for their good fortune, The Spillars and the good people of Mexia. They mounted their horses and rode from the ranch to the Convention Center feeling very humble, but blessed.

James was a ruggedly handsome young man, standing at six feet in height with black hair. He had deep blue eyes and carried himself in a confident manner. Bobby, on the other hand was slight of build, short blonde hair with hazel eyes and a sweet temperament that everyone loved.

When they arrived, the center was already crowded. A small band was playing among others songs, James recognized as "Dixie." A tear came to James' eye when he thought of his military buddies who were, who knew where, probably in Camp Chase Prison in Columbus, Ohio or Camp Douglas in Chicago. The boys felt so blessed to have survived the battle at Arkansas Post, the encounter at the Weatherby's Farm and the Indian raids into Texas. They had all the excitement they could stand for a while.

As they entered the building they spotted Mr. and Mrs. Spillar who motioned for them to come over to where they were standing. They then commenced to introduce them to the people in the hall. James and Bobby meet a lot of people but there was one who stood out. It was a little blond with blue eyes whom James felt was absolutely beautiful.

James asked Mrs. Spillar who she was and did she live in Mexia.

Mrs. Spillar said "James, you surely remember her, she's Laura Pruitt."

James replied, "Are you saying that's the little scrawny, freckled faced girl who was about this high (placing his hand about four feet off the ground) when I left for the Army?"

"That's her" replied Mrs. Spillar.

"Wow" was about all James could say.

The girl in question had grown into a beautiful and cultured young lady over the time of his absence.

He told Bobby "I think I'm in love."

Bobby laughed and said "You'd better get to know her before you ask her to marry you."

James blushed and said "She would never look twice at me; she could have her pick of any man she wanted."

The convention center by this time was full. People had come from as far away as Groesbeck, Fairfield and all the small hamlets in the region. They had a small band consisting of a guitar, fiddle, piano, harmonica and a bearded fellow blowing into a jug. The dances varied from the slow two steps and waltzes to the fast polkas and everyone's favorite, the square dance. After about thirty minutes into the gathering, Mr. Spillar moved upon the stage and he said he wanted to make an announcement. He said he wanted to honor the memories of those who had fallen in defense of the town. He said he felt a granite monument should be erected with their names inscribed on it. His family would purchase the granite stone with the cost of the inscriptions being borne by contribution from the citizens.

The citizens heartily agreed, with someone grabbing a small waste basket for the contributions. Mr. Spillar also said he wanted to thank each and every citizen for their unselfish acts and courage during this time of danger. And he said, "There are a couple of people who provided heroic action during this time of peril and should be recognized for their gallant accomplishments."

"Some of you will recognize these fellows since they worked on our ranch before they entered the service. Come on up and stand with me and let the citizens get to know who you are." As James and Bobby moved through the crowd to the front, Mr. Spillar was relating their experience at Arkansas Post, The Weatherby action and their riding for and securing General Sterling Price and his troopers.

Mr. Spillar placed the two boys at the front of the room and encouraged everyone to come forward and shake their hands. There were numerous young ladies who were not bashful in expressing their gratitude. James thought to himself, *all of this happened because his horse could jump higher than his father's back in Mississippi*. The world and lives hinge on, seeming at the time, small things.

# 19

## James Meets Wife

James did get a dance with Laurie Pruitt. As a matter of fact, she asked him for a dance. He was very surprised and he readily admitted he was not a good dancer. She said "That's alright, I'm not a good Indian fighter, but I can teach you to dance. And, I'll leave the Indian fighting up to you if that's alright with you."

These words Laurie spoke would come back with meaning in their future lives. James never became a "good dancer" but Laurie became, by necessity, a good Indian fighter."

The night passed swiftly and James asked Laurie if he could see her home. She readily agreed and James could not believe this was actually happening. He was quite inexperienced with the ladies, any ladies. He happened to think of an important consideration; he had no mode of transportation except his horse. Mrs. Spillar was standing close to the couple and told James if he needed a buckboard or buggy, they had brought a couple to the gala. If he needed one, he could take one of theirs and they could double up getting back to the ranch. She said they could tie

Charlie on their buggy and get him back to the ranch. He felt overwhelmed and it showed in his face. He looked into the eyes of Laurie and he knew, after so short a period of time, she was the one.

They had one more stop to make before they left the party. He had to ask Laurie's Mom and Dad if it was alright to take Laurie home. As best as James could figure, she was about sixteen or seventeen. She was probably about fourteen when he left for the war. That was going on four years. Those years had been good to Laurie as she had blossomed into a lovely young woman.

As they rode to Laurie's home, they stopped by a running creek with a gurgling spring. They were sitting in the buggy watching the water run over the rocks in the stream. James was nervous, no actually, he was scared to death. This was the first female except his mother or sister back home in Mississippi he had been alone with. He really did not know what to do or how to do it.

Laurie actually came to the rescue when she asked him if he had a girl when he left for the army. James decided to be completely honest and answered that she was the first girl he had been alone with in his whole life. She reached over and squeezed his hand and she told him he was the first boy she had ever been on a "kinda date", with or for that matter, had been alone with."

They sat and talked for almost an hour with the time flying by. Finally, Laurie stated she really had to get home or her parents would be worried. She reached over and clasped James's hand in hers and gave it a squeeze. He kissed her on the cheek and she turned and found his mouth. He was so excited he almost lost his composure. After holding their lips together for a moment, they both leaned back.

"Is that the way it's done?" James said.

"I don't know, but it was wonderful!" Laurie exclaimed.

As the horses hooves treaded through the creek water on their way to Laurie's home, they were making plans for a real date. Their future was uncertain as James would probably have to go back into active military service in the near future.

Of course, he had no commitment from Laurie, he had only driven her home from the convention center but he knew she was the one. And he felt confident that she felt the same way about him. He could not ask her for a commitment until he had some certainty in his life. By the time they arrived at the Pruitt Home, James was certain of what he wanted to do, but so much depended on the war.

When they arrived at Laurie's house, they sat in the buggy for an extended period of time talking about what the future might hold. James asked her if he might see her again and was Saturday night OK. She blushed and said it was fine with her but she would have to get her parent's permission. She squeezed his hand, just as she did at the creek and said she really wanted to have a real date with him. It would be her first date with a boy and she was glad he was the boy.

She reached around his neck and pulled him down to her lips and gave him a real kiss. She pulled away and said I'll see you next Saturday Night. If I can't go I'll get word to you somehow." James un-tied the horses from the hitching rail and drove home in a cloud. He didn't know much about love but something had a hold of him. On the way back to the Spillar Ranch, James could not ever remember the sky so blue and the stars so bright. All was right with the world.

When he got back to the ranch, he unhitched the team of horses and gave each horse some oats to eat and fresh water to drink. He noticed

133

that Charlie was in the corral and came running when James rode up. He had not spent enough quality time with his old friend but, he would take care of that from now on. He felt first-rate about his good fortune and how God had smiled down upon him and Charlie.

James had a hard time eating breakfast the next morning while Bobby pumped him for all the details of his time with Laurie. Bobby had also taken a girl home, but seemingly he was more interested in the romantic adventures of James than he was of his own. James told him most of the details, but there were some things he did not want to share even with Bobby.

James told Bobby, "I'm going to church today, we've got a lot to be thankful for."

Bobby said "If you go, so will I."

They finished their coffee and took a bath in the horse trough, put on the new clothes, including the new boots given to them by Mrs. Spillar. They saddled their horses and rode to the church.

When they arrived at the place of worship, they were greeted warmly by the congregation. They were made to feel as if they had never left to go to war. Reverend Jones welcomed everyone to God's House, mentioned the ones who had died in the defense of the town and the ones who so valiantly defended their friends and neighbors. He also mentioned the bold and courageous efforts made by Bobby and James to bring the army to the rescue.

The boys sat there squirming with embarrassment, but it felt good at the same time to be appreciated. James looked to the front of the congregation and saw Mr. and Mrs. Pruitt with Laurie, her little sister and brother. Laurie looked back at James and looked away quickly to avoid detection from her parents. Her little brother started pestering Laurie, he would look at and poke Laurie and at the same time, look back at James and laugh.

Thankfully, the minister started the sermon and her little brother turned to the front and left his big sister alone. The minister's sermon was appropriately entitled *"Thou shall not kill,"* the sixth commandant. This was a fitting subject after all the bloodletting that had occurred over the recent past.

James had a hard time personally, reconciling killing fellow human beings, with being a good person or Christian.

The minister started by saying "There are times when a humble and gentle person must turn the plow into a sword to protect oneself, family and neighbors." We have just come through one of these times when we had to take up arms to protect our property and the lives of our loved ones." "We do not take pride in doing these things, but on the other hand do not condemn ourselves for so doing."

After the service, James went over and engaged Laurie's parents in an extended conversation. Mrs. Pruitt was a school teacher and Laurie's Father was the owner of one of the general stores in Mexia. Their immediate plans for Laurie were a college education so she could teach school like her mother. Mrs. Pruitt went on to explain, in the frontier communities like Mexia, a college education was not a prerequisite, but it enabled a teacher to earn more money and get into administration quicker. James asked Mrs. Pruitt where Laurie was going to college. She told him that Tehuacana had a small but good institution of higher learning. She had hoped that Laurie could attend there.

James explained he had completed the tenth grade and had one more year to go to finish High School, but his folks had moved from Arkansas to Mississippi and he didn't want to back to Mississippi so he came to Texas. He was quite proficient in reading, writing and deciphering numbers (math).

James told Mrs. Pruitt "I've only known Laurie a short time, but I feel I've known her for my whole life. You and Mr. Pruitt should be proud, as she is a wonderful person. And, thank you for allowing me to drive her home from the convention center. Neither one of us has been on a real date before, but we have, with you and her father's permission, made a date for Saturday night. Hopefully this is not going too fast, but she is a wonderful girl."

Mr. Pruitt had been talking to other gentlemen in the church yard; however, he came over after a while, shook James's hand and stated how grateful he and his family were for their help in the Indian Uprising. Mrs. Pruitt explained to Laurie's Father about James and Laurie's plan for a date the following Saturday night. He was somewhat taken aback, but like all reasonable fathers, he knew this day would eventually come.

Mr. Pruitt said "Just take care of my little girl, she means so much to her mother and me."

James, with sincerity and honesty in his voice said, "I appreciate your trust and I will demonstrate it by treating her with reverence and respect."

He rode Charlie home as if floating on a cloud. After dinner at the main house, they rode out on the range to gather up as many of the scattered cattle as possible and bring them in for a count. Mr. Spillar was never sure of the number of cattle on the ranch since some were missed at round-up. They were basically checking to be sure the Indians had not killed a portion of the large herd and it had been overlooked on the causal check.

It appears that only a few head had been slaughtered for food. Indians preferred buffalo meat but they were in short supply in this part of Texas. It took a lot of meat to supply the needs of the number of Indians on this raid.

They spent most of Sunday riding over the nooks and crannies of the ranch until Mr. Spillar were pretty much satisfied that the majority of his cattle herd was still intact. His horses were in the corrals near the barns. The ones who were not caught and brought to the ranch house were taken by the hostiles. They loved their horses and were excellent judges of good horse flesh.

James asked Mr. Spillar "Don't you think we should check for brands on the Indian horses we have marked for extermination. We might find some of our horses in the Indian herd. Also, the other ranchers and stockmen should have the same opportunity. Even if we don't find their lost horses, they should be allowed to take what they can use. I guess I'm just a softie, but I hate to see good horses just killed. And, most of those horses appeared to be well-bred. Those Indians only ride the best horses they can steal."

Mr. Pruitt with a grin on his face said "James, you've got a good head on your shoulders; I think you will make a really good cowman."

Mr. Spillar and James were talking while their horses were slowly walking side by side. He asks James "What are your immediate and long term plans, if I'm not intruding? Both you and Bobby have a job and homes here as long as you want.

James replied "I honestly don't know what the future holds; the wild card is the War and going back into the Army."

James said he had been told by Bobby that he had a brief conversation with a trooper from a sister outfit who came through Teague the day he got back to the settlement. He was with the 10th Regiment, their old outfit, but from a different company. The man had escaped by simply walking away before they were herded into the boats. A lot of the men on the fringe of the battle lines (trenches) simply faded back into the trees and kept walking. He was able to procure a horse and got home pretty quickly. I didn't ask him to define procure."

He stated that he had been told that Colonel Nelson, their old regimental commander, was attempting to raise another military unit to go back and fight in the war.

James stated "I don't want to go back, but I feel it is my moral obligation to do so. I will not go searching all over the country, but if they do get organized and go back into the fray I will do so."

"For the time being, I'm going to work for Spillar Ranch, wear decent clothes, have three meals a day and sleep in a bed at night. I have met a wonderful young lady and I would really hate to leave Mexia until I know her better."

Mr. Spillars said, "Something I haven't told you, we lost our boy William or Bill as he was known. He died at the Little Rock General Hospital of disease. I know you knew him when you worked at the ranch, but he didn't join with the rest of the boys at Fairfield. He was a member of your company, "D" if I remember correctly."

James replied "I knew him at the ranch here, but, he was a Spillar and the cowhands didn't associate much with the bosses' family. I did get to know him pretty well while in the army. He became ill with the measles I think and they transferred him to a hospital. That was not that unusual as many of the troops were catching infectious diseases such as the mumps, measles, etc. and many of them were fatal. I had no idea that Bill had passed away, I'm so sorry."

Mr. Spillar said, "Thank you, I'm just grateful he had someone he knew with him when he became ill. It was and it still is, very hard on his mother."

As they looked up, the other ranch hands arrived. Mr. Spillar said, "We'll talk about this later and maybe his mother would like to be involved in the discussion."

James said, "Whatever you feel is appropriate, I owe so much to the family."

Mr. Spillar replied "We feel that you and Bobby are part of our family, especially you."

Bobby rode up to Jim and asked him "What are you thinking about? You appear to be deep in thought."

"I'd been discussing with Mr. Spillar about his son William who was in the 10th with us. He said he died in a Little Rock Hospital in October after he left the Camp."

Bobby said "I knew he contacted some disease, but I certainly didn't think it was that serious." He also lost two other sons during the Great War up to this date.

The Spillars have certainly contributed much to the Southern War effort. Jim said to Bobby "It's a hard life in a hard country. The women have to be as hard and tough as the men and sometimes I feel they are tougher." James said. He asked Bobby "are you going back in if another regiment is formed?"

Bobby looked Jim in the eye and said "I just don't know, I may go back, but right now I'm going home to West Columbia and see my folks. I haven't seen them in almost three years and I don't even know if they are still alive. They haven't been able to get mail in a long time and neither my Mom nor Dad is any good at writing letters."

"I'll go home, see about my folks and help them get everything in shape at the farm, have a visit and come on back Bobby continued." "If another regiment is formed, I'll go back in with you and if you've already left, I'll catch up. But, going home is something I've got to do, I hope you understand."

James replied that he certainly did understand. He would have felt badly if he didn't want to do it.

James told Bobby, "You should tell Mr. Spillars as soon as possible before he was assigned a rotation on the ranch." Bobby said he would tell him right after supper that night.

The world was moving swiftly for both of the boys. As a matter of fact, the boys were now men in age and experience. They were both twenty years of age and had spent three years in the army, fought Missouri Red Legs, Mexican Raiders and more than once had to combat the treacherous Redskins. And, Jim, as he liked to be called, had ridden all the way from Mississippi to the Spillar Ranch in Mexia, Texas. He liked to be called Jim since it made him feel like more of a grown-up.

The ranch work went well and he could ride over to the Pruitt Home to visit Laurie when she was not in school. Mr. Spillar was gradually giving him more and more of a work load and a little extra at the end of the month for the added responsibilities. He had been getting on well with both of Laurie's parents and Mr. Pruitt was treating him as a trusted son or member of the family.

Jim was happy, but he wished he could see his family in Mississippi. He loved them dearly and missed them a lot. Notwithstanding, if he had to be away from them, this would do well. He was seeing Laurie every Saturday night and having Sunday dinners with the Pruitts almost every week. Life was good!

# 20

## Honor Wins

One day while they were branding some new calves, one of the younger Spillars children rode out and told Jim, he was needed at the ranch house.  He told the men to continue and he would be back in a short while.  He rode Charlie to the main house and noticed several unfamiliar horses tied to the hitching rail.  He climbed the steps leading up to the porch and knocked on the door. Mrs. Spillar opened the door and ushered him into the big family room.

There were three men in military uniforms and they immediately turned toward Jim and shook his hand.  One of the men Jim recognized as his old regiment's commander, Colonel Nelson.  As a matter of fact, the 10$^{th}$ Regiment was also known as Nelson's Regiment.

Colonel Nelson was an old friend of Mr. Spillar and had come by for a visit.  He had been told by his old friend of Jim and Bobby's time with the 10$^{th}$ and their escape after Arkansas Post and their eventual trek back to their home at his ranch.  Jim did not actually, personally, know the Colonel because of the difference in rank.  Privates do not associate with Colonels.  It is called the non-fraternization rule.  It was not as adhered to as closely in the Southern Army as it was in most.

The Colonel asked Jim "What are your plans regarding your military obligation?"

Jim said "I intend to go back in if another regiment is formed."

The Colonel said "That's what I'm doing now, notifying you and men like you that you are needed to carry on the fight."


Jim asked the Colonel "What is the state of the army now?   It seems they and I mean the Southern Armies, have not had much good news since what a lot of people are calling **The High Tide of the Confederacy.**   The defeats suffered by our forces at Gettysburg and Vicksburg makes us wonder about our chances of success."

"I probably sound like a person with little love for my country and my country is the Confederacy.  In reality I love it more than ever, I just hope it's not a hopeless cause and all those young kids are not dying for nothing.  A saying that had a lot of reality in our unit went something like this; *it's a rich man's war and a poor man's fight."*  Tell me Colonel, is there any truth in that statement."

The Colonel was stunned but recovered quickly.  He said "They are all asking a lot of questions" "They know the chances of a quick or any victory is slipping away." "I'm not going to shoot someone who chooses not to continue but, I will continue, because it is the honorable thing to do."  "And, I might add I'm an honorable man." Jim spoke up and said, "That is the reason I'm going back into the Regiment."  "It is the honorable thing to do and if they don't have honor, they are not much of a country.

Jim asked the Colonel, "Have you set up a staging area for the men to come and sign up?"

"Yes" replied the Colonel, "it's in the same building where they signed up in 1861 at Fairfield."

James said "I probably would not have the same youthful enthusiasm that I had when I signed up the first time."

The Colonel replied, He understood, but he needed mature and serious soldiers, more than green kids.  He also asked Jim if he would be interested in a commission as a Second Lt.  Jim thought this over carefully and answered, "Yes! I would be interested."

A commissioned officer would stand a better chance in the future especially with the Pruitts and Laurie when he asked for her hand and he was going to ask for her hand in marriage before he left for the service. That would probably be a little selfish, but he had spent the last three years suffering deprivations consistent with Army life and he wanted a little happiness in his life and hers. He would ask Laurie to be Ms. Jim Walker and ride over to Fairfield on the following Monday.

If she accepted, it would be a short honeymoon, but short would be better than none. He asked Mr. Spillar for the day off so he could ride over and explain his plans to Laurie about their future and ask her for her hand in marriage. He could offer her more money and benefits as a commissioned officer than as a common soldier. He was, as he rode over to talk to Laurie, very excited but a little scared or nervous at the same time.

Laurie was still in school with this being her last year. Within a few weeks, she would be graduating from High School. Both she and her family were very proud of that. Few in the area had a high school diploma and with this certification she could teach in the public school system.

Jim reined up to the school and tied Charlie to the hitching rail. In reality, you really did not have to secure her to the railing as Charlie would not leave her position. He opened the front door of the small one room school house and got the attention of the teacher. She came over and asked James what he wanted. He told her he needed to talk to Laurie.

Laurie rushed over afraid that something had happened to her parents or others members of her family. Jim recognized the alarm in her face and told her everything was alright, he just needed to talk to her.

She almost yelled "What is it that makes you take me out of school in the middle of the school day?"

James just blurted it out "I'm going back into the army!" He explained that Colonel Newton, his former commander, was putting together another regiment and he was going to join up. A look of surprise and anguish shown on her face and she said "Why? I thought we had a future right here in Mexia working for Mr. Spillar or even my Dad."

"Laurie, I love you more than anything, but I have a moral and ethical obligation to fulfill my commitment to the army I don't think you would think much of me as a man if I didn't do the honorable thing. Honor is sometimes the only thing a man can look back on and be proud. And Colonel Newton has offered me a commission as a Second Lieutenant. Laurie, that is huge as it will mean so much to us after I get out. I love you so much and even the Colonel said he didn't feel the South could hold out much longer."

"Oh, I almost forgot the most important question I came here to ask, will you marry me?" Laurie almost fainted as Jim grabbed her and held her tight. This was a lot to hit her with all at once.

She said "Oh Jim that would make me the happiest girl in the whole wide world but how?"

Jim replied, "The way I've got it figured, with the permission of you and your parents, we can get married Saturday night and have a short honeymoon for a couple of days until I have to leave for the army."

"I've thought about this being selfish on my part, but I could whip the whole Yankee Army if I knew you were home waiting for me. We need to get started as soon as possible. Can you get permission to get out of school for the rest of the day?　We need to check on the parson's schedule and the availability of the church. Also, we need to talk to your parents so it doesn't appear we're doing this behind their backs. One more thing, you may take two or three days out of school, but you are going to finish school."

"Okay!"　Laurie exclaimed, "Oh Jim, I'm so excited, and you're making me the happiest girl in the world."

"Then, go tell your teacher you're going to be absent for a few days, we need to check with the minister and talk to your parents. Talking to your parent is a chore I don't look forward to. It hasn't been that long since I asked your dad to allow me to take you home from the convention center."

"Someday, we'll have a daughter who some young man will come courting and I would certainly have a hard time feeling anyone would be good enough to fancy my girl."

Laurie, as she started back to the door to enter the school building said "We've got to get busy or we'll never make the deadlines."　As she came back out of the school, she told Jim to remove his foot from the left stirrup as she placed hers in the foot support and swung up behind him and said, "Let's go." I think it would be a good idea to go see Mom and Dad first, okay?"

When they arrived at the Pruitt home, Laurie asked Jim "Do you want me to go in first and explain what they're doing?"

Jim replied, "No, we'll do this together. If we are going to be a team together we might as well start acting like one."

Mrs. Pruitt was at home but Laurie's father was still at his business in town. Laurie decided to tell her mother and maybe she could help break their plan to her Father.

Much to the surprise of both prospective newlyweds, Mrs. Pruitt didn't act surprised and seemed to warm to the idea quickly. She said they had suspected that something was brewing. They both wished Laurie had finished school and had gone on to college before marriage.

Jim spoke up quickly and said, "We have decided she is not going to quit school and hopefully can live here as she is now since I'll be back in the military. I have been offered a commission as a Second Lieutenant and that should help us later in life. And, I'm hoping the war will over by the time the school year is out and we can start our new life without being concerned about fulfilling my military obligation."

Mrs. Pruitt asked if they had gotten in touch with the pastor yet.

Laurie said "No, that was their next stop."

Jim said "We'd better get a move on before he schedules something else."

"You kids hurry to the pastor's home and I'll tell your father." Her mother told them.

Laurie exclaimed, "Oh Mother would you? I was dreading that so much. I love you more than you will ever know."

Laurie's mother called out and told her to take the buggy or saddle her horse, riding behind Jim was not ladylike and they were not married yet. Laurie went out to the corral and called Old Braze over and put on a bridle. She then put on her saddle and mounted him, demonstrating her skills as a champion rider. Old Braze was a five year old blaze faced gelding that Laurie had raised from birth. She would put her riding skills against any boy in the area.

They arrived at the reverend's home just as he was arriving from an appointment. Jim greeted him and asked if he and Laurie could have a few minutes of his time? They both apologized for being there without an appointment but something important had come up. The reverend said his job was to help and what could he do for them?

Laurie blurted out "We want to get married and we want you to perform the ceremony, will you marry Jim and me?"

Laurie went on to say "we want a Christian ceremony and hoped it could be held in your church."

The minister said "The church is not mine, it belongs to the Lord. When do you plan to have the wedding?"

Laurie said, "Saturday night, if possible. You see, Jim is being reinstated with $10^{th}$ Regiment and will leave next Wednesday."

"Have you talked it over with your parents?" the minister asked.

"Yes, we have and they wished the circumstances were different but they understand. I'm going to continue to live with my Mom and Dad and attend school until the war is over."

The Reverend said "Jim, you haven't said anything, is this something you want and agree to?"

"Oh yes Sir, I've discovered the girl has a good head on her shoulders and can make sound decisions on the fly."

The reverend kinda smiled and said "Every successful man has a smart wife, and a smart husband listens to her. Ordinarily, I would require a young couple to attend a counseling class before they make such an important decision and even though it happened quickly you seem to know what you are doing. The quantity of years in your age are just numbers, it's the caring you have for each other that's important. Never go to sleep each night without telling the other you love them."

"Well, when did you want this event to happen?" asked the minister. They told him they were hoping they could schedule the wedding for Saturday night since Jim had to leave for the army the next Wednesday. The minister said "Saturday will be fine as there is nothing planned to date."

The minister asked almost as an afterthought, "How old are you, Laurie?"

"I'll be eighteen next month" answered the bride to be. "Will I need some consent form signed by my parents?" The minister said with a smile, "maybe in New York or Boston but not here in these frontier settlements.

What else do we need to do? James asked.

"Probably a million things but we need to talk to both your parents and I would like to discuss this with your surrogate parents, Mr. and Mrs. Spillar." Laurie said "I would like to go see the Spillars first to give my Dad a chance to maybe cool down about our decision, Okay?"

They rode up to the main house, walked up the porch steps and knocked on the front door. One of the younger Spillar children opened the door and hollered out "Mom, Dad, its Jim and some girl."

Mrs. Spillar came to the door and said "Jim and Laurie, it so good to see you both." We've just sat down for supper and we've got plenty. Won't you please give us the honor of dining with us?" Jim looked at Laurie and Laurie looked at Jim and finally Jim said he really needed to talk to her and Mr. Spillar.

They walked into the dining room with the big long table filled with kids and happy faces. Mr. Spillar rose from the table to greet the two younger, unexpected guests. Mr. Spillar said I knew you had a good head on your shoulders and having Laurie as a friend proves it. We've known Laurie all her life and she is a wonderful person."

Jim replied "We need to talk to you and Mrs. Spillar about an important decision Laurie and I are making."

"Since my parents are in Mississippi, I've kinda adopted you as my surrogate parents, I hope you don't mind and we both value your opinion. We are going to be married on Saturday night. It is not going to be a big wedding, but we would like for you, Mr. Spillar, to be the best man and Mrs. Spillar to be the bride's maid." The Spillars looked rather startled, but quickly recovered and answered almost in the same instance, "We'd be honored."

They told the Spillars of their plans for Laurie to finish school while Jim finished his military obligation. Jim said he hoped the war would be over soon, but it did not look good for the Southern Cause. He added that he had decided to take his commission as a Lieutenant for the extra pay and benefits now he would be supporting someone other than just himself. He chuckled and commented he wasn't so sure just how much the confederate money would buy."

They said their goodbyes to the Spillars and Jim took Laurie home. As they were riding up to the Pruitt home, they saw her father in the front yard.

Laurie said "uh oh, Dad's home, let's get this over with."

Mr. Pruitt called out to them as they rode up, "Jim, you and Laurie come on into the house; I need to talk to you." They tied their horse to the hitching rail and walked into the house with Laurie meekly trailing behind Jim. Mr. Pruitt said "I understand from my wife you kids are planning on getting married and setting up housekeeping."

Jim replied "Not without your permission and blessings." He related to Mr. Pruitt "the state of affairs about him going back into the service, their separation and they loved each other very much."

Mr. Pruitt shook Jim's hand and told him "If we're going to lose my daughter we're both glad it's to you. We wish you had more time to do these things, but it seems you don't. I understand Laurie is to continue living with us while you are in the army, is that correct?"

"Yes sir, we want her to finish school while I'm away. This is not the way we wanted it to be, but the circumstances dictated our timetable. And, thank you for being so under-standing, I love you as if you were my flesh and blood parents."

Mr. Pruitt asked Jim about his parents, where they lived and would they be at the wedding?

"No, they live in Mississippi and I have not seen them in over four years. I love and miss them very much but the distance and the war make it impossible for them to be present; I hope to introduce their new daughter-in-law to them in the near future." Jim went on to say, "The Northern Forces are occupying where they live making visiting them very dangerous."

Mr. Pruitt said he hoped this war, which was supposed to have lasted only a few weeks, would be over soon.

Jim in excitement asked "What day is it? "We have a lot to do before Saturday Night."

Mrs. Pruitt said "It's Thursday Night." Mr. Pruitt shook his hand, Mrs. Pruitt embraced him. He put a light kiss on Laurie's forehead; both Laurie and especially Jim felt a little awkward displaying affection toward each other in the presence of her parents. The parents said as Jim was going out the door, "We're glad to have you in the family."

Jim rode home on a cloud. He had never before felt this complete. In the beginning, he never felt Laurie would speak to him that he was not good enough for her and now she had consented to be his wife. "God was good." He went to bed in the bunkhouse, but sleep was slow in coming, he was just too excited.

When he was going to the cook shack for breakfast, Mr. Spillar called him over and told him "If he had something to do to get ready for the wedding, just take off and do it."

Jim replied, "No, I think everything is done that we can do for the present."

Jim rode out with two other cowboys to do some branding, fix some patches in the fences and change out some leathers (gaskets) on a couple of windmills. It was difficult to concentrate on anything except the wedding, Laurie and their life thereafter.

A little thought was given to going away with the military again. He really didn't want to do it. And, he wondered about Bobby. He had not heard from him and he had been gone for an extended period of time. He prayed his parents were okay and he had not met with some misfortune. There was no way to contact him or Bobby's parents as West Columbia was a considerable distance from Mexia. Bobby was the best friend he'd ever had and he worried about his safety and that of his parents. He simply did not have the time to go to West Columbia before his wedding and his leaving for the army.

That afternoon, he rode over to the Pruitts to see Laurie. She had actually spent the day in school. She said "I just needed something to occupy my mind." "I'm so excited, I can't sleep or eat and all I think about is you and our life together."

"Yeah, I know, all I can think about is the most beautiful, gracious and intellectually girl in the whole wide world and she is going to be all mine tomorrow night. I have to pinch myself to make sure I'm not dreaming."

He stayed rather late talking to Laurie's parents, just getting to know them and them know him. They were wonderful people and what was so wonderful was they actually seemed to like and accept him. As he was riding back to the Spillar Ranch he knowingly rode Charlie across a prairie far from the ranch house and worshiped God in His natural cathedral with the full moon and every star in the heavens out and shining. Sitting in the saddle on Charlie's back he talked to God, thanking him for blessing him while being so undeserving. He said again "God is good."

Saturday finally arrived with most of Jim's day was spent taking a bath, a haircut, shaving and making sure the clothes would fit. Mrs. Spillar had come up with a real "suit and tie" and even some socks and Sunday shoes.  He looked like a real Slicker with all the *"Sunday Go to Meeting Clothes"* on and he felt pretty special, but scared.

# 21

## Marriage & Bobby

Mrs. Pruitt still had her wedding gown and with a little "taking up" and "letting out" it fit Laurie just fine. Laurie was so excited, being able to get married in her Mother's gown. Jim and Laurie didn't expect much of a crowd, just close relatives and a few friends; however, the church was standing room only. Jim had saved some money while working on the ranch and used some of it to buy Laurie a wedding ring. Mr. Spillar was there to act as the best man and Mrs. Spillar was there to act as the bride's maid. As they walked down the aisle, Jim glanced briefly over to his right, he saw a familiar face, and it was Bobby.

Jim said to himself, "Thank You, God. All is right with the world." The ceremony was over quickly and every man from the state of Texas kissed the bride and shook Jim's hand, telling him that he wasn't good enough for her. At the end of the line was Bobby. He said he was sorry he hadn't gotten back sooner but his parents needed his help and he wasn't completely convinced he would go back into the army again.

Jim told him of Colonel Nelson visiting and recruiting for a new regiment and he had offered him a commission if he would go back in for the duration and he had agreed to go back for the time period. Jim continued, telling Bobby he knew the South had little or no chance, but to him it was just a thing of honor. And, maybe a little bit might be attributed to his opportunity to become an officer.

Jim offered, "I feel he would give you the same offer if you were to go back in."

Bobby said "I'm just not sure, I've given three years to the military and I don't think they have a snowball's chance in hell of winning and, my folks need me in West Columbia."

"I'll go with you to Fairfield next week and talk to them, but I won't promise anything at this point. I don't have that sense of honor you do about this. I feel that I have fulfilled my commitment, as have you, with the three years we served fighting for the South."

Bobby was going to stay in the bunkhouse and try to decide what to do. Mr. Spillar offered him his old job back or he could stay there until he decided one way or the other. As for Jim and Laurie, they rode off in a buggy furnished by her parents with a large "Just Married" sign on the back with strings of tin cans trailing behind. Jim was concerned about scaring the horse due to the noise generated by the cans.

The Pruitts had a mother-in-law house behind the main house which was used by Mrs. Pruitt's mother until she passed away. This was to be their honeymoon cottage and they were so grateful. For the purposes of good taste, the night will not be expanded on except to say it was the most blissful period in the lives of both Jim and Laurie.

They both got up in time to grab a bite of breakfast and make the Sunday school and the church service the following morning. Jim sat in the pew and thought to himself, *I don't deserve this, Thank you, Jesus."* Jim and Laurie both answered the invitation and rededicated their lives to God. Jim had been saved at a young age in Mississippi before moving to Arkansas. Laurie had been saved at approximately twelve years of age. They both felt it was good to start fresh "together."

After the church service, the Spillars invited everyone out to the ranch to honor the newlyweds and have a social before Jim went back to the war. They had, in the great house, a large room especially designed for large social functions and at times to entertain their ranch hands. And, of course, the newlyweds were the guests of honor. Jim thought to himself *I've got a lot to live up to.*

In the middle of the afternoon, they bid everyone goodbye, got in their buggy with the sign and trailing cans and went back to their house for some time to be alone. The time together would be limited and they wanted to make the most of what they had left. Supper that night was served by the Pruitts and shortly after the meal; they excused themselves and said they were going to turn-in early.

A rooster crowing woke Jim as he cradled Laurie in his arms. He kissed her on the lips and said, "I love you today more than I did yesterday but less than I will tomorrow."

She looked up in his eyes and said "Just think, when you get back from the army, we'll wake up every day just like this, I truly love you."

Jim said "I've got to hurry and get over to Fairfield. I don't want to do it but it's something that I'm honor bound to do, I hope you understand."

She said "I especially don't like it either, but I understand."

"I'm going to meet Bobby in front of the livery stable at nine; he is going to ride over with me and talk to Colonel Newton about going back in. He really doesn't want to go, but he will give the Colonel an opportunity." They dressed and hugged, ate and hugged and then he went out and saddled Charlie and rode off to town.

Bobby was standing beside his horse when he saw Jim riding up. He said "You're early, did she kick you out already?"

Jim replied with a grin, "She would have to do a lot of kicking to get rid of me." As Bobby got on his horse, Jim asked him if he had decided anything about going back in. Bobby answered that he really hadn't, he wanted to see what was offered and then he could decide.

The approximate twenty miles to Fairfield went relatively quickly, talking to Bobby about his time in West Columbia and what he was going to do if he did not re-enlist. He also remembered the first time he made this journey to sign up at the start of the conflict. His attitude was completely different as he was young and seeking glory. He did not then understand the horrors of war and the needless waste of young lives. General Robert E. Lee once said, "It is good that war is so horrible, for fear that they might grow fond of it."

# 22

## Military Calls Again

When they arrived in Fairfield, there were a lot of young men standing around the courthouse. Some of them were vaguely familiar, probably from their times as members of the $10^{th}$ Regiment. Jim and Bobby dismounted and asked a couple of men where Colonel Nelson's office was located. They said they were not absolutely sure, but they thought it was on the second floor of courthouse.

They thanked the men and entered the front door of the building. Upon entering they saw a large sign that read "$10^{th}$ Texas Infantry, second floor. And, after climbing the stairs, Bobby said, "Well, I think we've found it." Toward the back of the room sat Colonel Nelson in his Confederate Uniform. When he saw Jim and Bobby, he stood up and waved them back.

Colonel Nelson said "It's good to see a couple of familiar faces again. I know we did not associate with each other before; however, I did know who you were and kept close tabs on you two and as many of my enlisted men as possible. The non-fraternization rule will not be in effect particularly between Jim and me." This brings to a point I need to cover with Bobby, "What are you going to do, Bobby?"

Bobby looked perplexed and said "I really don't know what to do.   I have parents in West Columbia who are getting old and need my help. And, I don't have the appetite for war that I had when I enlisted before. I feel the fortunes of war have turned against the South.   Not many of my friends I enlisted with are still alive and the ones that are alive are in prison camps.   I know this can be construed as treasonous statements, but nobody loves the South more than I do and I have given a lot to her, as has Jim.   I don't know if it gives me the right to make these statements, but feel it's time for some honest discussions.

The Colonel stated, "You're simply articulating what most of the people of the South, both soldiers and civilians feel.   I can't say I don't have doubts, but my honor, duty and responsibility to the men in my regiment far outweigh my own personal considerations. "

"Bobby", added the Colonel, "they are willing to offer you a commission as a Second Lieutenant. To be completely honest with you, I wasn't at all sure I would offer you the commission until you just spoke your mind.   I want and the army needs officers who can and will think for themselves. I'm thinking you have the good sense not to go around giving your candid opinion to just any and everyone."

Colonel Nelson said "Its lunch time. Let's eat lunch and you can give me your decision then." And, he added "Jim I'm assuming you're going to take your commission?"

"Yes Sir, I am!" Jim replied.

Colonel Nelson said "Jim, you will be assigned as Platoon Leader of "C" or Charlie Company and if Bobby decides to join I will assign him as Platoon Leader of "B" or Bravo Company. Most members of your unit will be ones who escaped like you   al Arkansas Post."

Jim spoke up and said, "I don't think I will know these men on a personal basis. Most of my friends I served with are either dead or in Camp Douglas Prison in Chicago, I shouldn't have any problem with being too close to guys I was friends with when I served in the ranks."

Bobby was sitting there with a serious look on his face when he spoke up, "Colonel, If I can receive a commission, I'll sign up and I will do my very best." "The colonel, with a big smile on his face said "Well, that finished out my officers.

Bobby, you will be the Platoon Leader of Bravo Company and Jim will be the Platoon Leader of Charlie Company. We hope to have a complete compliment of troopers by next Monday."

"Most of these men will be re-treads who have served before. That means they will not have to spend much time on close order drill or other basic training procedures. My plans are to have the ranks filled, weapons and equipment issued and ready to march by next Monday. That means you must be here for reveille Saturday morning at 6:00 AM. You've got the remainder of this week to take care of any business at home and say goodbye to your loved ones."

Jim asked, "I don't mean for you to divulge any secrets, but do you have any idea where we will go and what we will be doing?"

The Colonel said, "I'm not sure, but I have been told that a contingent of Yankee Troops was trying to link up with General George Thomas' troops at Nashville. General John Bell Hood with the Confederate Western Army will be attempting to prevent this consolidation somewhere around Springdale or Franklin, Tennessee, just southeast of the State's Capital at Nashville. This is important, so go home and report again either

Friday Night or early Saturday Morning in time for muster."

Bobby and Jim bid their commander goodbye, walked outside the courthouse, mounted their horses and headed west toward Mexia. They rode in silence for the first few miles then Bobby asked Jim. "What have we gotten ourselves into? If what the colonel said is true, this could be a very rough campaign. I'm assuming that they will be traveling by train at least part of the way, that's a long way to march."

Jim replied, "Bobby, I'm glad you'll be with me. You know I love you like a brother or probably closer than a brother. We've been together for a long time and survived some really tough action, but I just hope I didn't influence you to do something that could cause you harm."

"Jim, I'm a big boy now, just turned twenty-one, and besides, they are going to make me *an officer and a gentleman.* All joking aside, if we survive this, I think it will good for us. Anything that is worthwhile has some danger or effort combined in it."

Jim and Bobby rode on silently to Mexia deep in thought of might lay ahead. Jim, when they got to the outskirts of Mexia asked Bobby to go home with him and sample what prompted his marriage

172

to his wonderful new wife, her cooking. Bobby said if it wouldn't be too much of an imposition, he would like that. He said he had no idea when he would have an opportunity to have a home cooked meal again. He added that even when he was home, his mother was in ill health and he had to do his own cooking.

When they rode up to their home, Jim walked up to the front door and Laurie met him at the open door, threw her arms around him and kissed him hard and hungrily.

Jim said, "Whoa girl, we've got company." Laurie looked beyond Jim and saw Bobby standing there will a sheepish grin on his face. She, with a somewhat embarrassed look, said "Bobby, please forgive us, I thought we were alone."

"No! No! Forgive me." Bobby quickly replied, "I can see why Jim is always in a hurry to get home."

Jim, as he pulled out of his wife's clasp, asked her if it was alright for Bobby to share supper with them. They had both agreed to go back into the army and Jim emphasized **both** which indicated Bobby was going too. Laurie smiled and told Bobby she was glad he was going with Jim they could take care of each other.

The meal was spent visiting and talking about life after they returned home. After complimenting Laurie on her fine meal on such short notice, Bobby said again "I understood why Jim was so smitten with you."

"Bobby, don't go far, you would make a good backup for Jim." Laurie laughed.

The next few days flew by. They were spent making a simple will for them both and just spending time together. They would go every evening to the creek where they stopped on their first date. It was a wonderful time in their lives and as is always the case, it ended much too soon.

It was understood that Laurie would live with her parents and continue her education. She was scheduled to graduate from high school in the spring and start college at Tehuacana in the fall. Jim felt good that Laurie would be in such capable and caring hands. Everyone loved Laurie.

Jim and Bobby left before sundown on Friday night so they would have plenty of time to get to Fairfield and make the 6:00 reveille on Saturday Morning. There was a mixture of apprehension and excitement in Jim as he said goodbye to Laurie, mounted his horse and rode off to Fairfield. He left Charlie with Laurie, and rode off to Fairfield.

They arrived a little after midnight, unsaddled their horses and laid their bedrolls on the courthouse lawn. Sleep was difficult due to the excitement and over the recent past, he had become used to sleeping in a feather bed. Sleeping on the ground wasn't as exciting as he remembered it.

Jim woke up as the eastern sky lightened with first rays of the morning sun. The smell of freshly brewed coffee was invigorating and refreshing. The company cook had a large black pot brewing the coffee; he grabbed a cupful and waited for the early morning wake-up call. Jim had almost finished his second cup of coffee when Colonel Nelson stepped out and attempted to outline some type of workable formation.

One has to remember these were farm boys, ranch hands and sometimes soldiers he was trying to work with and were not professional soldiers. They might not have had too much military discipline, but their ability to fight was never in question. Most of the men or boys, as they were, had prior military training with their basic problem being organizational cohesiveness. This could only be overcome with working together over time. Time was something that currently was in short supply.

They worked hard for the next two days selecting enlisted men for the various needed rolls such as platoon sergeant, squad and fire team leaders. The company was woefully short of personnel, but for the time being had to work with what they had. By Monday morning, the organization and its ability to act as a cohesive unit were better. However, it still needed work, "lottsa" work.

# 23
## Marching Orders

Monday morning after first formation, the troops were marched down to the rail station and loaded aboard box cars. These were categorized as 40 X 8 meaning they could carry forty men or eight horses. There were roughly forty men to a car, very uncomfortable and hot. One of Jim's men sitting close to him said "It may be hot and uncomfortable, but it beats the hell out of being hot, uncomfortable and walking."

The trains would stop every couple of hours for a "Pee" break and thirty minutes for food breaks. The route selected was one which was to avoid northern troops and went through Shreveport, Jackson, Mississippi, and Birmingham, Alabama and on to Columbia, Tennessee. As Jim found out later, the unit was to come together at Columbia, Tennessee with a combined attack on Franklin and later on Nashville.

It took them almost three days and nights to reach Columbia and they had to wait two more days for Hood's Army to arrive. The weather was cold as it was in the deep fall with snow mixed with sleet falling both day and night. Camp fires were dangerous since they could be seen for great distances, but sentries were posted and the men were cold. Again, these were Texas Cowboys who simply were not used to this type of weather. Late in the morning of the second day after arrival, Hood's Army came tramping up the Pike leading to Spring Hill.

They did not stop but kept marching as if they were not there. It seemed that anyone who was anyone marched by them that day. The Texas Unit stood at attention when Generals Hood, Granbury, Cleburne and Forest came by on the Pike. That was not all but it was all that could be recognized from their position

The troops wore tattered and frayed clothing with dilapidated footwear or no shoes at all, but their spirit was something to behold. They might not be invited to a classy ball but they had a lot of fight left in them. They were going to a "dance" being hosted by General George Thomas, the Rock of Chickamauga.

General George Henry Thomas was a Virginian who did not go with his native state but fought for the Union. He gained his "nickname" during the Battle of Chickamauga when he remained on the field of battle and prevented a total collapse of the union lines. He and 30,000 Union Soldiers were hosting the dance at Nashville.

However, several thousand union soldiers were behind them, being led by General John McAllister Schofield, trying to link up with General Thomas at Nashville. The fly in the ointment for the southern forces was they were between the forces of General Thomas and General Schofield and they couldn't afford to let them link up. This did not promise to be a fun time for either participant, but especially the South.

As the last of General John Bell Hood's Army marched, Colonel Nelson's Texas boys fell in behind them on the pike. They arrived in Spring Hill about nine o'clock and bedded down as best they could in the wooded area off the road. Colonel Nelson said there was a Northern Army coming up the road behind them but they would post sentries and skirmishers to prevent being surprised.

Bobby and his platoon bedded down close to Jim and his troopers. Once the men were down and company guards were posted, Bobby and Jim tried to get some rest as they knew tomorrow would not be a fun day. About two o'clock in the morning, Jim was awakened by someone shaking him and saying to him "wake up, wake up" Jim became alert from a sound sleep, it was Bobby.

Bobby said "Jim, there are thousands of men marching by on the road, are they our troops?"

Jim said, "I wouldn't think so, remember they were the tail end of the column this afternoon, there was no one behind us."

"I think we should notify someone, but who?" replied Bobby.

Jim said he would wake up Colonel Nelson and "He will know to whom to make the report."

Bobby replied, "Do you know where he is and how to get to him without being shot?"

Jim said, "If the entire northern army can march by on the open highway and not be challenged, I should be alright."

After a diligent search, Jim came up empty. He could not find Colonel Nelson or anyone with authority to take appropriate action. If this was General Schofield, this could mean big trouble for them the next day.

Schofield and his army marched by without being challenged. This was a colossal mistake and would cost the lives of countless men of the Southern Army in the coming battle.

# 24

## The Battle of Franklin, Tennessee

The next morning after a sleepless night, Colonel Nelson called a meeting of his officers and told them he had spent the night at General Hood's Headquarters. He said "After much discussion with some of it bitter, a plan of attack was formed with their unit being attached to General Granbury's Regiment. They would be attacking the middle of the Yankee line near the Carter House." No one was comfortable with General Hood's plan with Generals Forest and Cleburne being the most vocal. Colonel Nelson said General Forest had to be forcibly restrained from physical attacking General Hood. He said "Hood had accused, among others, Patrick Cleburne and Nathan Bedford Forest, of being too scared to fight." He added further." "That's two men you don't accuse of being cowardly."

That's when Colonel Nelson, for a second time, told his officers in the meeting that the 10th had been attached to General Granbury's Regiment and they would be involved in a frontal attack in what appeared to be a very well fortified position. He continued to tell them that Granbury had a lot of Texas boys who had reputations for being real scrappers and added that they might know some of these boys from back home.

"Write your letters do whatever you need to do and get ready to shove off. We are scheduled to start the assault at 9:00 sharp. I'm not going to blow smoke, this could be very unpleasant. We will be going in somewhere between the main house and the cotton gin." Colonel Nelson added. "Some of those boys dressed in blue, according to some of the scuttlebutt, are armed with repeating rifles."

"This is what Forest and Cleburne were concerned about, "attacking men with that much firepower behind well fortified positions."

General Patrick Cleburne had been at odds in the past with Hood. Hood had implied that Cleburne was a little slow to lead his men in heavy combat. He also had alluded to this fact about Forest. He, Forest, had to be restrained from physically attacking Hood. The meeting calmed down and the battle lines were drawn. This was against the voiced objections of many of the officers present.

General Cleburne and Forest were the best generals in the Southern Army and probably the preeminent in either the North or South. Neither generals had attended the accepted military schools, e.g., West Point, VMI, etc. which almost every military leader, either Union or Confederate, had gone to. Cleburne had been in the Irish Army before coming to America and Forest had something like a couple of years of formal schooling.

Forest never studied tactics at West Point, but in the ensuing years, Forest's tactics would be taught at West Point. Cleburne was a dentist and operated a dentist office in Little Rock, Arkansas. Forest was a self-made millionaire through investing and the slave trade. Both Forest and Cleburne joined as privates and rose through the ranks. Most of the Southern Army felt that Cleburne should have been at the head of the Western Army instead of General Hood. General Forest was promoted to Lieutenant General, but by that time, it was too late for the Southern Cause.

Colonel Nelson attached his company to General Granbury's unit with orders to attack the center of the line. Bobby's last words to James, with a big smile on his face, were "I should have gone home to West Columbia." With that they fell into their respective positions and headed northwest following the order to "close ranks."

The Battle of Franklin, Tennessee was absolute chaos. Afterwards, a thousand bullet holes were counted in the Carter House alone. Except for a portion of the northern army who were issued repeating rifles there was no time to reload. The armies were fighting in close combat using bayonets, their rifles as clubs, rocks or whatever could be used as a weapon. It was complete and utter chaos.

The battle cost the lives of six generals and Bobby. Both Generals Cleburne and Granbury, with roughly 7,000 troopers were killed. Jim saw Bobby early in the fight charging hard toward the northern trenches.

The Yankees pulled out early the next morning and headed for Nashville to link up with General Thomas. The Southern Forces gathered their wounded, buried their dead and got some order in their state of confusion. Jim found Bobby at the far reaches of the field of battle within ten yards of General Granbury.

General Cleburne was found dead on the field of battle with his weapon, boots and most of his uniform taken by battlefield scavengers. This was not a fitting end to a great man. Jim carried Bobby to a large oak tree and buried him there in its shade. He marked the tree so he could find it later and hopefully bring Bobby back to Mexia to his parents in West Columbia.

Jim was heartbroken, but he was a soldier with duties to perform. He really didn't feel that "honor bound" to a lost cause, but he had a sense of obligation to his men. He had to make sure the wounded were cared for and the ones that were healthy, organized for their trek to Nashville to meet with General Thomas. It was a meeting that Jim was not looking forward to. He was glad to be alive, but he felt as most of the other troopers did, disheartened and disillusioned. The war was lost and people were dying for no discernible reason. Most of the men, including him, just wanted to go home.

Jim counted heads and found that roughly fifty percent of his platoon was dead, wounded or captured, with Bobby's platoon approximately in the same fix. He gathered the surviving squad leaders together and asked if they would be willing to combine their men with his to form a full strength platoon. They all agreed and fell into a platoon formation to march on to Nashville. These were heartbroken men leaving friends behind, underneath unfriendly sod. Tears flowed freely on their cheeks as they headed down the pike.

Colonel Nelson asked Jim and his platoon to act as a rear guard for the Southern Army. He felt this was the Colonel's way of giving some relief to their unit. They had been hit hard with any relief welcome. They were on the tail end of Hood's Western Army of the Confederacy. The leading forces were already encountering the federal defenses in Nashville. The results of this encounter would be the same as that faced at Franklin with more killed, captured and wounded. The young men who had given so much for what was now a lost cause were once more marching toward battle with no hope of victory. It was sad on one hand and a statement of honor on the other.

The battle was fought with the inevitable outcome: A victory for General Thomas' Northern Army and more casualties and defeat for the Southern Cause. Jim's platoon was spared heavy combat being in the rear. By the time they reached Nashville, the outcome was inevitable.

After the battle, General Hood tendered his resignation and it was accepted. Most of the surviving units that were somewhat intact went on to fight for other units in the East and the South. The Southern Troops were disillusioned with their commander and many just went home.

The troopers wrote a parody to one of the most popular songs of the South "The Yellow Rose of Texas." "You can sing of your Clementine and sing of Rosa Lee, but General Hood of Texas played hell in Tennessee." Jim left Nashville with most of his unit intact and was considering going home for the second time in the war. He had a heavy heart, leaving Bobby in Franklin, but he was anxious to get back to Texas and see Laurie. It had not been a long time but it seemed like a lifetime. Colonel Nelson had gone east to fight with General Joe Johnston in the Carolinas.

# 25

## Going Home Again

Jim had offered to make the trip with the Colonel but he told Jim, "Go home and see your wife and take care of the home front. The war will be over in less than six months." He added. "Lee can't hold out much longer without food and ammunition and Johnston will encounter General Sherman on his march from the Georgia Coast to Richmond." With some finality, "It's just a matter of time. Go home and protect your family, they will need some protection from the scalawag and carpetbaggers who will show up at the end."

He stated he had no idea what type of governmental control would be instituted after the armistice. "Would the high ranking officers be considered traitors and shot? There was no question, the war was lost but how would the defeated be treated was the question?"

Jim called his men together and explained the situation. He offered to release the men who wanted to go with the colonel and continue the war to the bitter end or they could march with him as a unit back to Mexia. Not a man left the ranks to go with Colonel Nelson. Jim told his men they would leave at 6:00 AM the next morning and walk back to Texas. Jim did a head count and came up with twenty-five troopers.

They needed horses badly. Being from Texas they were all good riders. The prospect of walking several hundred miles to get home was not a reassuring thought. Jim called the men together and asked them about the prospect of making a midnight raid on the Yankee Depot to requisition some of their four legged mounts to   get back home.  The men were enthusiastic about the prospects and a plan was formulated.

Jim told his men "In all likelihood the horses would be lightly guarded with the men on guard duty not that diligent since they figured the battle was over and the rebels would be like a ghost slinking away.  We really don't want to fire our guns for obvious reasons including the prospect of bringing down the whole Yankee Army on us. And, we don't want to hurt anyone unless we have to."

At about 10:00 PM, the troopers darken their faces and other exposed skin and marched off toward the Yankee encampment under an overcast sky. The troopers had trouble seeing the men in front of them until their eyes became used to the darkened environment. They had no trouble getting through the enemy's lines as they were enjoying the spoils of victory, including some spirited drinks.

Jim with a hand signal motioned for his men to gather around him. He said "The horses are just ahead and lightly guarded." He added, "I want the three guards surprised, gagged and tied up. He stressed that they were not to be overly rough with them unless it was absolutely necessary. The rest of the troopers would go into the stables and saddle as many of the horses as possible and ride like hell to their campsite."

He said "he didn't want the rustling to be discovered until the next change of guards which is around 2:00 AM." "This should give us enough of a head start to keep ahead of the Yankees, who had been celebrating most of the night before and were probably groggy, headed.

When they got back to their camp, they hurriedly divided up their horses, saddles and other accruements and headed south. They rode hard until they felt comfortable with stopping and resting. One of the troopers said "these horses were big, stout and had stamina but, he still preferred the quarter horses out of Texas. These horses remind me more of a plow horse than a riding horse. "Yeah, but they remind me of riding in a rocking chair," one of his buddies quipped.

The band of troopers skirted the larger settlements and stopped at the smaller southern settlements for food and water. They stopped in clumps of trees and thickets and slept in shifts. No one ever got more than four hours of sleep. They traveled both day and night. Their biggest problem was crossing large bodies of water such as the Mississippi, Arkansas and the Red Rivers. They were fortunate enough to find ferries that had sympathy for the Southern Cause that took them across these bodies of water. They had some Confederate money, but everyone knew by this time that the money was not worth the paper it was printed on.

The boys were traveling through the state of Tennessee, Mississippi, and Arkansas and into Texas. They had to be careful as the Yankees had large Yankee contingents in these regions. The troopers made it back to Texas with little or no problems. The civilians in these areas would hide them, feed them and put them up in their barns for overnight stays. They also would make them aware of the location of the Yankee camps and directional movements.

They were not treated as conquering heroes, but rather the civilians seemed to convey sincere appreciation of all their efforts. These survivors had little need for back slapping, flag waving or glory. They had lived like animals for the South while fighting the war and simply wanted to go home and lead as regular a life as the conquerors would allow. But these people were very helpful and appreciative. Jim and his men conveyed their gratitude for their caring attitude and assistance.

They crossed into the Lone Star State at Texarkana and rode south. The trees had lost all their leaves and the weather was cold. Even so, the boys were warm in their hearts as they were home and it felt good. Several of the boys left the group in the northern part of the state since their families lived in Denton, Fort Worth, Weatherford, Waco and Ennis. What was left of the group that had left with Jim at Fairfield was now filled with joy and sorrow.

Jim was full of sorrow as he had left his best friend in Franklin, Tennessee. He blamed himself for Bobby's death since he put a lot of pressure on him to reenlist. Jim had to ride down to West Columbia and talk to his parents and explain where and how he died. But that would be at some point in the near future. Tonight, he would see his wife. Seeing and telling Bobby's parents about their lost son was not something he was looking forward to, but he felt that was the least he could do.

He was overjoyed, on the other hand, to be almost home and holding Laurie in his arms again. God had been so good to him to allow such a woman to be his wife, his very own. He rode through Teague on the way to the Pruitt's home in a melancholy mood. He simply could not get the thought of Bobby out of his mind.

By the time he arrived in Mexia, it was a cold night with misting rain mixed with sleet. Laurie was still in school but was out for the Christmas Holidays. She was still living with her parents in the small house behind the main house as far as Jim knew. The ground was frozen, with the horse's hoofs hitting the frozen ground making noises which could be heard from a long distance. Jim couldn't decide whether the noise from the horses hooves were louder than his own beating heart.

# 26

## Home Again

He was so excited, but apprehensive also. He was anxious due to his appearance, his clothes were ragged, his hair and beard needed trimming and all in all he was not the clean cut young man who Laurie married and sent off to war just a short time ago. He could have gone by the ranch and borrowed some clothes and cleaned up, but he was anxious to see Laurie again. He rode up to the porch, tied his horse to the porch railing and walked briskly to the front door. He knocked on the door and waited. He could hear someone walking across the living room floor and suddenly the door open and there stood Mr. Pruitt.

He didn't recognize Jim at first until he told Mr. Pruitt who he was. He embraced Jim and pulled him into the interior and hollered for Laurie. Mrs. Pruitt and Laurie both came running into the parlor and stopped and started crying. Laurie ran and jumped into Jim's arms and starting kissing and crying, crying and kissing. Everyone seemed to be overcome with emotion. It was a touching moment.

Laurie kept repeating, "Is it really you? Jim, is it really you?" After a while, they settled down a little and talked somewhat rationally. Mr. Pruitt said "We really feared the worst as we had heard of the horrific battles in Franklin and Nashville. We had heard that was where you went after you left here. Jim, we thought Laurie was a widow before she really became a wife. We were really fearful."

With tears rolling down his cheeks, Jim replied, "yes it was a horrible encounter; the worse I have ever seen. I lost over half of my platoon there, including some very good friends, as well as Bobby. I'll always feel to blame for his death as I feel responsible for talking him into reenlisting.

Laurie cried out, "No, No, not Bobby! I loved him like a brother."

Jim told the Pruitts, but especially Laurie, "I've got to take a trip to West Columbia to meet with his parents and explain how he died. I buried him under a large oak tree near Franklin and marked the tree, so I could find it again. I intend to go back and retrieve his body after the war and bring it home for burial.

Mr. Pruitt asked "What now? When do you have to go back?"

Jim answered Mr. Pruitt, "I really don't think I will go back. The South is spent. I think most of the leaders know it's over and are looking for a way to end it honorably." Jim, with tears flowing added, "I pretty much knew it was over before the Battle of Franklin but I was hoping for a miracle and I wanted to be an officer. What a price to pay!"

Jim said "I'm so sorry to talk about nothing but doom and gloom and I must look a mess. We left Nashville, traveled through Mississippi and Arkansas to get back into Texas. We had to dodge Yankee Patrols all the way. We didn't have the time or the wherewithal to clean-up, shave or change clothes even if we had any to change into. But we are so happy to be home and to have someone to come home to."

Mrs. Pruitt told Jim, "Jim, take a bath in our bathroom and you can use Laurie's daddy's shaving equipment just this once, can't he?" she asked her husband?

"Of course, he can! Afterwards, I'm sure the kids will want to spend some time alone together."

Jim kissed Laurie again, thanked the Pruitts and went into the bathroom. The bathroom had a large oversized bathing tub with hot water, added courtesy of his lovely wife. While the water was heating, he shaved his face and cut his hair with a pair of scissors and Laurie's assistance. The warm water felt wonderful, it had been a long time since he had actually bathed with soap and water.

While he was soaking in the tub, Laurie laid out a change of clothes and underwear on the bed. Jim was so tired, but when he saw Laurie standing beside the bed he felt energized. He came into the room, grabbed and kissed her fully on the mouth, with Laurie having to restrain him. She said "Whoa boy, we need to see Mom and Dad for a little while, eat supper and then afterwards, we'll go to our house in the back. You go talk to them while I clean up the bathroom and cook some supper, Okay?"

Mrs. Pruitt went to help Laurie cook the meal while Mr. Pruitt asked questions about the war including "Would the Yankee Military occupy as far South as Mexia?"

Jim answered "Yes, they were roaming south across the Sabine and Red Rivers with battles at Sabine Pass and Galveston. To tell the truth, there was little to stand in their way."

Jim continued, "The war was over for all practical purposes except for the continual dying and suffering of the hapless soldiers. The generals who don't have to suffer the horrible condition of the private soldier make the decisions to quit or continue the conflict."

"The battles of Gettysburg, Vicksburg and Chickamauga pretty much depleted the South of their fighting men. The battle of Chickamauga was technically a southern victory, but they lost men there they couldn't replace. The Yankees can replace their casualties, the South cannot. It is simply running out of resources, most notably men. The old truism "It's a rich man's war and a poor man's fight" is descriptive of the present situation."

"Lee cannot adequately feed his soldiers or arm them any longer. Jim continued, "General Johnston is wandering up and down the East Coast and putting up a good scrap from time to time, but it will have no lasting effect. And, General Hood has resigned as Head of the Western Armies. As I stated, the war is over for all practical purposes, but it will drag on for three or four months causing additional heartache and suffering. I think it is now a habit, a very bad habit, but no one wants to admit they are whipped, but they are. Some, if not most of the officers and non-commissioned officers, literally don't want to give up their power, the power of literally, life and death over their men."

Mr. Pruitt asked Jim, "What will be our fate as civilians?"

Jim said, "All I hear is scuttlebutt, but if Lincoln has his way they will be welcomed back into the union with open arms." But on the other hand, there are fire breathing Yankee politicians who want to make us suffer. I just don't know and no one else does. I do pretty much know the slaves will be freed and given the right to vote and only those white men who can prove they did not take up arms against or provide comfort for the south will have the right of suffrage. That will give the Blacks a lot of political power and control."

Just as the conversation got heated, Mrs. Pruitt walked into the room and said, "The meal is ready." Jim, who had not eaten or slept on a regular basis for what seemed like months stood up quickly and followed her into the dining room. He sat down rather timidly after he realized he wasn't eating at a military mess. He quickly rose to his feet and waited for everyone else to be seated and ask the blessings.

Mr. Pruitt asked Jim to "give thanks" and he did in a simple but heartfelt manner. Jim was thankful and also hungry. He had to be careful because he was not used to dining with civilians. The meal was delicious and much appreciated. In his exhausted state, the food made Jim very aware of his fatigued condition. He actually dozed off while eating Mrs. Pruitt's meal.

Mrs. Walker, now that had a ring to it! Mrs. James Jefferson Walker had slipped out while they were fixing supper and fired up the wood stove in their little house so it would be warm later. She helped Jim to his feet and guided him to their little home to the rear of the main house. When they entered the structure, Jim said, "I've waited for this moment for what seems like an eternity." He then sat on the bed and reached for Laurie. He then lay across the bed and passed out.

Jim did not move a muscle until eleven the next morning. It took a while before he realized where he was. He, first of all, thought he was in the army and was attempting to remember where he was and what he was doing. He then looked across the room and saw Laurie sitting in a chair in the corner of the room patiently awaiting his return to the conscious world. When he did remember and realize, he was overwhelmed.

He motioned for Laurie to come to him and apologized for his inability to stay awake. She gently put her open hand over his mouth and told him how much she loved and at the moment needed him. Jim was awake and soon was in wonderland. Their lovemaking was over much too quickly, and Jim and Laurie's thoughts were to stay in bed all day. But this was not to be as Mrs. Pruitt was calling and stating that lunch was ready.

# 27

## End of War/ Reconstruction

The next few weeks were a blur. It took some time for Jim to get used to civilian life again and Laurie to get used to married life. It took a while for everyone to get used to what the people in the South termed "Reconstruction," the term given to the occupation and guidance provided by the Northern Armies. Reconstruction was an almost untenable arrangement for the occupied states.

The carpet baggers and scalawags had free rein with the law authorities being the ones who were appointed, not elected. The ultimate authority was an occupying military unit who did not want to be there. They had little sympathy for the Southern people whom they had fought for the past four hard years. Of course, most of the troopers were decent young men who just wanted to go home. But there was a segment that took advantage of their power and committed dreadful acts. There was usually no one who would take any action to punish these offenders.

This was a situation that existed all over the South. The rascals who perpetrated these acts knew they were above the law. The acts ranged from petty theft, disrespecting women, to murder with little chance of persecuting them in a court of law.

Lt. General Nathan B. Forest and a small group of men in Memphis devised a plan for an organization called the Ku Klux Klan or KKK to maintain some degree of order with midnight raids by hooded private citizens. If one of the unregulated hoodlums, under the protection of the Union Army, committed some unlawful act, they could expect a visit from the local clan on a dark night not too far in the distant future. It worked well until it became corrupted by local toughs and rednecks. General Forest served as the head of the organization until it ceased to be a law enforcement organization and turned into a self-serving association that was largely racist in character.

Jim had been home for almost six months when several acts of a loathsome nature were committed around Mexia. Mr. Spillar had consulted with the military commander about these incidents but had basically been rebuffed. He then called a meeting of the local male citizens of the Mexia Area. Mr. Spillar opened the meeting, explained their predicament and asked for ideas. After some suggestions, Jim said he had heard about General Forest's action in Memphis and brought it up at the meeting.

Mr. Spillar asked Jim if he had been involved with the organization at all. Jim answered, "No, he had never met General Forest. He said, he had seen him at Spring Hill, Franklin and Nashville, but he had never conversed with him on a personal basis." He said "He had talked with some troopers who served under him." They said, "He believed that what they're experiencing now could be a problem after the war ended." He offered, "That some sort of secret organization without the sanctioning of the occupying force would be needed to maintain order during the inevitable occupation.

One of the men sitting toward the back asked how it would work. Jim said he was no expert, but if someone committed an unlawful act or disrespected a woman, the culprit could expect a visit from the hooded organization in the dead of the night. Jim added, "It seems to be a workable solution to what could be a real problem." The men were impressed with Jim's knowledge and Mr. Pruitt succinctly reminded the men in the meeting that Jim was an officer in the Southern Army. Jim added, "They will be completely at the mercy of the local commanding officer." Jim continued, "The way they are treated will completely be at his discretion."

The war, for all practical purposes, was over in April, 1865 with the surrender of the Army of Northern Virginia by General Lee at Appomattox to General Grant. It took a couple of months to rein in fragments of armed forces to make the surrender complete. It was a time of bedlam and disorder in the wake of President Lincoln's assassination, the fire eating Northern Politicians had now all the ammunition they needed to treat the rebel states with an iron hand. No one in the North had much or any sympathy for the South. Only time would tell the type of control that would be exercised by the occupying forces at Mexia.

A committee was appointed with Jim acting with authority to organize the group and report back the following week. The group was charged with taking action against culprits who seemingly were free to commit acts with impunity. Jim reiterated that they didn't know if this was actually going to happen, but they had to be ready and prepared to protect the citizens if it should occur.

Jim told the committee, with all present, "That a meeting with the commander of the occupying army to make him aware of the fact that a clandestine organization would be available to protect the local citizens, if necessary!"

The following week, a company of the 5th New York Calvary arrived, commanded by Captain Will James. The unit used the convention center for its headquarters and called a general meeting with the town folks to acquaint them with what would be expected. At the meeting, the captain seemed to be a reasonable person who hoped the period of reconstruction would soon be over and they could all go home. He stressed that if the citizens would be reasonable everything would be fine.

Jim walked up after the meeting and introduced himself and asked for a private meeting. Captain James readily accepted the opportunity to become more familiar with the town and its citizens.

Captain James said "Why not now?" We can go into my office and discuss items that will probably come up during this period."

Jim agreed, "That would be good." We need to get to know each other as quickly as possible. "I was an officer in the Confederate Army and understand some of the limitations you face. But, we've heard of atrocities suffered by other jurisdictions without fear of any chastisement.

And, we understand the South lost the war, but we only ask for protection of those who can't protect themselves." Jim added, "Being on a field of battle is one thing, but to cause harm and humiliate civilians is intolerable."

"We are willing to subjugate our lives for a period of time to pay reparation, but we will not stand by and allow low rent soldiers, scalawags and carpetbaggers to disrespect our women or cause harm to the young and infirmed."

Captain James answered, "This will not happen on my watch. We will take what actions are necessary to make sure of that."

Jim said "That makes me feel relieved that you feel that way, the citizens are very worried, especially after some of the stories that they have heard from other jurisdictions."

Captain James asked Jim, "Have you considered putting together a secret organization to enforce the rules to protect your citizens?" The captain went on to say "It's not something that I could know about or condone, but if I were in your situation I would seriously consider it. I know it works well in other parts of the South."

Jim was taken aback by his statement and the overall attitude of Captain James. "Just between you and me, we have considered it and as a last ditch effort, we are willing to try it." Jim went on to say, "It works a lot better with supportive and perceptive military leaders like you, Captain James."

A meeting of the committee was called and all agreed that an organization should be formed. No mention was made of the conversation between Captain James and himself. This could be a very serious stain on the Captain's military record. And, because of this candid conversation and cooperation between the parties, no serious breaches occurred during the occupation.

Jim had assumed his old job with the Spillar Ranch, except now he was the second in command under Tom. He was known as the Assistant Foreman. He enjoyed his job and he had just found out that Laurie was with child. This was joyous news that made his chest swell. He was continually thanking God for his blessings.

The young couple had purchased ten acres from Mr. Pruitt and had commenced saving for a home of their own. Jim and sometimes Laurie spent as much time as possible clearing their new land and placing their new home site. Life was relatively dull based on Jim's previous four or five years. Jim came to realize that his past action experiences could not compete with the joy of waking up beside and just living with Laurie and their new son, whom they named Joshua.

Time passed quickly with Jim spending one term as Mexia's Intern Mayor. The elected mayor had a heart attack and could not fulfill his official duties. Jim said later, "It was a good experience, but he was glad to get back to punching cattle." By this time, Jim and Laurie had their home built and a little girl all their own named, Ruth. The name was gleaned from the Bible as was Joshua. Life was good!

In the winter of 1871, tragedy struck. An epidemic swept over North Texas, killing countless people, including the beautiful Laurie and their precious Joshua. Jim and little Ruth were sick but they overcame and survived. Jim was simply devastated. He would not come out of their house for many weeks. He had witnessed many tragic deaths during the battles of the war and engagements with the Indians, but this was different. Laurie was his life. He would never get over her death. Little Ruth was too young to comprehend the finality of death. For the first few months, she was always asking "Where was her Mommy?" Jim would simply say Mommy has gone to be with Jesus. Mr. and Mrs. Pruitt tried to help, but they were in a state of shock as well.

Laurie and Joshua were buried under a giant Oak tree behind their home. It was a constant reminder of what he had lost.

# 28

## Bringing Bobby Home

Jim planned to go back to work after a couple of months, but before he did, he took that promised trip to West Columbia. He asked the Pruitts if they would look after little Ruth while he completed some unfinished business. He really felt bad about not going to visit Bobby's parents as he had promised to do. It seemed like yesterday but it had been over five years. He didn't know if they were still alive or not.

He also promised to bring Bobby's body back to West Columbia. Now was an excellent time to do it. He could take a train from Fairfield to Nashville and on to Franklin. He could rent a wagon in Franklin and go on to where he had buried Bobby. He still had a crude map of the location which he had kept in his dilapidated uniform since the battle. He had some money Laurie and he had saved for an emergency over and above funds they used for day to day expenses of living.

Jim knew nothing about transporting a body hundreds of miles and needed help from an expert. He went to see Claude Johnson, the owner of the local funeral home and asked his advice. Mr. Johnson said if the body had been in the ground for five or six years, there probably would be a lot of decay. He asked if the body was wrapped or preserved in any way. Jim replied, "He was buried on the Battlefield at Franklin, Tennessee." Jim said, "I wrapped him with the only thing I had which was an army blanket. "Well," replied Mr. Johnson, "take a sleeping bag that will zip up and wrap the body with some type of leak proof material and wrap it securely, place it in casket or wooden box which can be placed in the baggage car. Also, fill the container that holds the body with moth balls. That will keep the smell down and help preserve the body."

Jim took Little Ruth over to his in-laws and told her how much he loved her as did her Grandparents. He caught a train at Fairfield and began his long journey to keep his promise to Bobby and himself. It took three days to travel the distance from Fairfield, Texas to Franklin Tennessee. This time included the time for switching and waiting for other trains to pass.

When he stepped off the train at Franklin, it looked nothing like he remembered it before and after the battle in November of 1864. It had been cleaned up and restored. Jim went to the sheriff's office and showed them his hand drawn map. He asked if they recognized any of the terrain or features on the map. He said, "I remember it was near a cotton gin and the Carter House." Jim added, "It was where Generals Cleburne and Granbury were killed in the battle." The Deputy gave him the address and directions to a historical society who would probably know the exact location. As he was on foot, he asked the deputy where he could rent a wagon and team. He would need the wagon to transport Bobby's body back to the railway station.

The direction given by the deputy was good and he found the Historical Society with little or no trouble. The lady who was behind the counter of the historical society was very helpful and didn't ask if the body belonged to a soldier wearing a blue or gray uniform. She told Jim, "The body or location seems to be on the south end of the Carter Place. That appears to be where the fighting was the most horrible." Jim said, "I think I will recognize it because I buried him under a large oak tree with his name carved in the trunk." Jim asked, "Is there anyone I need to get permission from to conduct the search and dig up the body?" She said, "I don't think so, nevertheless if you are questioned; tell them to come see me."

"Oh by the way, where are taking the body and what is his relationship to you? She asked Jim.

"He was my friend, a really close friend. I'm taking him home to his parents in West Columbia, Texas." Jim continued, "That's a small town approximately fifty miles southwest of Houston. I'm taking him home to his parents." With a tear in her eye, she pointed Jim in the right direction and watched him go out the door.

Jim untied his team, climbed into the wagon and tried as best he could to follow the lady's directions. The cotton gin and the Carter House were easy to locate and the landmarks were coming back into focus. At the crest of the small hill ahead of him looked like the large oak tree. This could be where he had buried Bobby's remains. He popped the reins on the back of the team of horses as they broke into a trot. *I think this is the spot he thought.* As he pulled up beside the tree, he could make out some crudely carved letters which appeared to be Bobby's name.

Just as he was getting down from the wagon, a rider on a palomino came up the hill and said, "Hey, wait up a minute. Who are you and what are you doing here?"

Jim said, "My name is James Walker; I was a Lt. with the 10th Texas Regiment during the battle of Franklin in November, 1864. I'm keeping a promise to a friend who died fighting with General Granbury's Brigade." Jim continued, "I buried him the morning after the battle under this tree. It still has his name I carved in the bark; can you see it?

The man said he was a member of the Carter family and he lived in the house down the hill and to the north. He said, "The heaviest fighting was in this vicinity." Jim said, "I know, I was here." "We suffered over fifty percent casualties; it was a pretty good scrap." The Carter family member said he was sorry for Jim's loss and asked if there anything he could do to help. Jim said, "No, I just have to dig him up and get him back to his parents in Texas. However, I do appreciate your kindness."

Jim had some blankets in the wagon but not the other items necessary to transport the body back home. He remembered he buried Bobby about three feet deep in relatively soft dirt. He was hoping the ground was still pliable and after a couple of spades of dirt, he discovered the digging was pretty easy. It finally hit James this was Bobby and he lost all control and unashamedly wept with his head resting on his knees.

This was not fun, this was Bobby; he was not uncovering a sack of potatoes. After about thirty minutes his shovel struck something solid. Jim got down on his hands and knees and starting to dig around the bundle with his hands. It was Bobby; Jim was digging and crying, crying and digging. After another half hour, he had the corpse loaded into the wagon, encased with two blankets and a large army quilt.

Jim hurried back to town and found an undertaker. He asked him about a wooden box or a cheap casket. The undertaker said they had readymade pine boxes which they used to encase the casket as it was lowered into the ground. It would be the cheapest way to go. Jim asked if he would help him put Bobby into the pine box. But he wanted to put him in a sleeping bag, place him in the pine box and fill the box with moth balls. Jim asked the undertaker "Is there a hardware store in town or somewhere I could get moth balls?

For whatever reason, the undertaker had a large inventory of mothballs and also had a rubber container to fit bodies into. They put Bobby into the enclosure and zipped it up. They then placed him in the wooden box and filled it with moth balls. Jim could not believe his good luck having all these goods and services at one place. The undertaker said it was not unusual as they shipped a lot of the victims exactly as they were Bobby.

Jim paid the undertaker, but the charges were minimal. There was lot of sympathy for the fallen at Franklin. Jim thanked him and drove down to the railway station to get Bobby into the baggage car. They were going home. He was fulfilling his promise he had made so long ago. Jim thought to himself, *I hope his parents are alive and can appreciate his return. He can spend eternity with them.*

The return trip was pretty uneventful having to change trains twice at Little Rock and Dallas. After Dallas, the next stop was Houston, where he off loaded and rented another wagon and team for their last leg of the trip to West Columbia roughly fifty miles south by southwest.

West and East Columbia are twin settlements sitting on the Brazos River near the mouth, as it flows into the Gulf of Mexico. Jim was aware of the historical significance of the settlement as numerous signers of the Texas Declaration of Independence lived there. Jim didn't think he would have a lot of trouble finding the Johnson homestead in a settlement that small. Nevertheless, Jim didn't know if Bobby's parents were still alive.

The trip from Houston to West Columbia was uneventful but pleasant giving Jim time to reflect on his life from the time he arrived in Mexia to the present time. It was springtime with the flowers blooming, the trees budding and the wild life running wild before him. He knew it seemed selfish to be so grateful and full of life with Bobby's lifeless body in the back of his wagon. The road led through Alvin, Angleton, crossed the Brazos River just before entering West Columbia. Just a couple of miles past the river were the outskirts of the settlement.

Jim pulled into a trading post, tied his team to a hitching rail and walked into the store. The woman behind the counter was friendly and her name was Mrs. Lily Thompson. She was a pretty lady probably in her early fifties with grey streaks in her blonde hair. She then asked if he was from West Columbia. Jim answered and said, "No, he was from Mexia and he was looking for the Johnson Place." She said, "The Johnsons, an older couple had a place about a mile north of town." However, they had both passed away within a month of each other. They are buried in the town's cemetery, located about a half-mile down the road on your right, the north side of the road.

She looked Jim over from head to toe and she said, "You're not their son they kept looking for, are you?" Jim said, "No, but I've got their son in the back of the wagon out front. I was bringing

219

him home to his parents. It seems I'm too late. Is there someone I need to obtain permission from to bury Bobby in the cemetery?" She said, "Yes, there is a person and I'm that person. What happened to their son?"

Jim said with tears in his eyes, "He was killed fighting with Generals Granbury and Cleburne at the Battle of Franklin, Tennessee. I buried him and marked the grave so I could bring him home someday.

"Are you telling me you went all the way to Tennessee and brought the body back so he could be near his parents?"

Jim replied, "He wanted to be with his mother and dad and I had promised to do everything I could to make that possible."

Mrs. Thompson was overcome with emotion with her tears flowing down her face. She said, "If I remember correctly, there is space beside Mr. and Mrs. Johnson's graves to place their boy." She raised her voice and called for her husband to come to the front and mind the store while she took Jim to the cemetery.

Jim helped her upon the seat of the wagon and started through the settlement to the graveyard. The site was not large since the settlement was not over fifty years of age. The markers denoting the Johnson's Graves were cheap and non-descript with space on one side for Bobby's resting place. Jim told Mrs. Thompson he would have to dig the grave, if she would mark the correct spot.

She said, "They have a working group that does that for local people."

Jim said, "No, I will do it as a labor of love. If someone wanted to help, that would be gratefully accepted."

Mrs. Thompson said "Take me back to the store and I will get you some help."

By 2:00 in the afternoon, the grave was dug and most of the townspeople had gathered to pay their respects, thanks to Mrs. Thompson. She had also contacted the local minister to conduct a religious memorial for Bobby. It was nice.

After the service, Jim stayed with Bobby and with reverence said his last goodbye. With tears in his eyes he turned his wagon toward the store and slapped his reins down on the back of the horses and headed into town. He could stay in town long enough to take care of Bobby's business or Mrs. Thompson and the Reverend seemed to be willing and able to attend to the final details.  He wanted to know if there was any cash that could be squeezed out of the homestead, primarily to purchase an appropriate headstone.

Jim thought a headstone which covered all three plots with the mother and dad's names on the top center and Bobby's in the below center would be nice.  This would cost a sizeable amount.  If there was no money in the equity of the home then Jim had agreed to pay for it.  Mrs. Thompson said she felt certain the money could be raised, hopefully from the sale of the homestead and if not, from the pockets of the local citizens.  "After all, the reverend reminded the crowd there in the store, he gave it all, fighting for our way of life, at Franklin, Tennessee."  There was not a dry eye in the house.

Jim left his address with Mrs. Thompson and told her to write from time to time.  He told her, he really appreciated what they had done for Bobby and his family.  He then climbed into the wagon and headed north toward Mexia.  He had no idea what he was going to do with the rest of his life.  He was a widower with a young girl child.  His lust for life and excitement had greatly diminished since he had lost Laurie.  His world was gone, but he had to keep going for Little Ruth's sake.

# 29

## Life after Laurie

He turned in the wagon and team at Angleton and took a train on to Fairfax. He counted his chips on the way home. He had a good job, a beautiful little girl and his whole life ahead of him. Laurie would not want him to just give up. He decided to make a concerted effort to get back into the main stream again.

He had read in a newspaper of good cheap land near Fort Chadbourne in Runnels County approximately two hundred and forty miles west of Mexia. He asked Mr. Spillar if he could have three or four weeks before he went back to work. He also asked the Pruitts if they minded keeping little Ruth a while longer. They said "Of course, they didn't mind, it kept their mind occupied so they didn't think about Laurie all the time." He didn't tell them he was thinking about moving somewhere else. It was just too difficult there in Mexia where everything he saw reminded him of Laurie and their past life.

He left bright and early Monday morning and headed west toward Runnels County. It was a bright, cloudless, almost summer day, a day that makes you glad you are alive. It was a day like so many spent with Laurie during their time together. He was riding Charlie for the first time in a while. He used the Spillar horses in his string doing the ranch work. Charlie was what one called "semi-retired."

The trees were just beginning to "bud out" with the first flush of spring time. Texas was a beautiful state, especially during this time of the year. The animals had not enough exposure to the human species to be afraid and played joyfully all around Jim as he rode west. The first large settlement he encountered was Waco, with the Brazos River running inside its corporate limits. Waco was basically the genesis of the 10$^{th}$ Texas Infantry, Jim's old military unit.

Jim stopped at the general store and asked if anyone knew Colonel Nelson? The older lady behind the counter said she knew him, but she didn't know if he was back from the war. Someone standing close by said he heard that he and a few of his troops had found General Forest near Selma, Alabama and had fought with him. Jim told the small crowd that had gathered that he had released them at Nashville and told them to go home. The war was lost, but Colonel Nelson was honor bound to continue the fight until the formal surrender.

Someone said he had a place where his wife and children lived on the outskirts of the settlement and he should go by and see them. They said news was scarce with mail almost non-existent due to reconstruction. Using the directions given him, Jim found the commander's home. It was a simple, but impressive dwelling with everything in its rightful place.

Jim tied Charlie to the hitching post and climbed the four steps leading to the porch and front door. He knocked on the door and a petite and distinguished looking lady opened the door and said, "I'm Mrs. Newton, may I help you?" Jim told her who he was and that he was simply there to express his gratitude to her for her husband's tutelage, help and to see if she and her children were alright. And, Jim wanted to know if she had heard from him. He told her he had not seen or heard from him since the battle of Nashville. She seemed to be legitimately stunned to see someone from her husband's unit. She quickly asked him to come into the house and offered him a cup of tea or coffee. He told her coffee would be good, if it would not be a bother.

She said "No, it was such a joy to meet someone who had served with her husband and had seen him recently."

Jim told her, "I have not seen him since he released my unit at Nashville. At that time, he was in excellent physical condition and still dedicated to the cause."

She said had not received any specific information since the end of the war. This was sometime after Lee had surrendered at Appomattox roughly two years ago. Some of his colleagues had sent word to her that he was captured, attempting to smuggle the Confederate President, Jefferson Davis, out of the country to freedom. No definite word was known as to the prison but she was confident by the available information he was in good health and would be released soon. Dedication and devotion has a price and Colonel Newton was paying his share.

She asked me in an uncomfortable manner "Are you still dedicated to the cause?"

Jim really did not know what to say, but replied "Well, I haven't thought the war was winnable since the summer of '63, after our losses at Gettysburg and Vicksburg. The battles at Franklin, Nashville and others were a useless infusion of blood, and depleted our country of it greatest resource, its young men. I think we should turn our weapons into plow shares and cease killing our young men, both north and south, on the field of battle. The victors were decided some time ago, but they keep sacrificing our men in an unending caldron of death."

He added "I'm sorry; I sometimes get carried away with the senselessness of the war. I know Colonel Newton feels the same way, but he will not vent his true feeling in front of his subordinates."

General Lee was supposedly heard to say "It is good that war is so terrible for fear that they would learn to love it." Jim said.

"I'm afraid too many of our leaders from both sides have learned to love it too much. Your husband is not one of these men; he is caught up in the whirlwind of the war. He just feels an overwhelming sense of responsibility to his oath and his men. He is a legitimate hero who puts his men and responsibilities first; otherwise, he would be home with you and his family."

Jim detected a tiny trickle of tears at first and then the flood gates opened. Mrs. Newton quickly sat down in an easy chair and Jim handed her a handkerchief in which she buried her face and let her emotions out. He felt very uncomfortable on one hand since this was Colonel Newton's wife, but on the other hand, he wanted to hold her and give her some degree of reassurance that everything would be alright.

Just then a young man came running into the room asking "What's wrong Momma? Has something happened to Daddy?"

"Oh no, baby, this is something that has been building up for a long time. This is Mr. Walker, who was a lieutenant in your daddy's regiment. He just came by to pay his respects and hopefully learn of some news of your father. The crying was something I just couldn't hold back any longer, my pent-up emotions just came bursting out. I'm so sorry for my outburst."

Jim said "A good cry is good for the soul and if anyone has a right for a good cry, you do."

"Mr. Walker, this my son Wayne and he has a sister named Dorothy who is somewhere in the house. Wayne is fourteen and Dorothy is ten years of age. They haven't seen their Daddy since the fall of '64 and very little since the war began. They miss him so."

Mrs. Newton asked Jim to lunch with the hearty endorsement of her children. He was concerned about the imposition of cooking and the lack of food since the war had exhausted everything. But he agreed to eating lunch and it was enjoyable spending some time with a real family again. I felt very comfortable with Mrs. Newton and her two children. It felt like he had known them all my life.

Mrs. Newton asked if Jim was married and he told her about Laurie and their two children. When he told her about Laurie and their little boy passing, she started to softly weep again.

He told her "It was very sad still and it was still very hard for me." Friends told me "It would get easier with time, but it really has not up to this point." That was the reason he was going to Runnels County; because everything back home at Mexia reminded him of his wife and family."

Mrs. Newton told him he should check with the county sheriff to see if the passage was clear. There had been some real problems with the Indians between Hamilton and Brownwood. The Indians knew that the armies both North and South were fighting each other and very little time could be devoted to the Indian problem. They had pretty much free rein in the area of killing and raiding.

After lunch, they talked for a while and Jim told her he had to go, but he would like to talk to the county sheriff. Mrs. Newton said she really felt that was a good idea. She had heard the Indians

229

were even more abundant farther west and the sheriff would know.    He gave Mrs. Newton and the kids a hug telling them how lucky Colonel Newton was to have such a wonderful family.

# 30

## Trip to Runnels County

He went out on the porch with a little bit of a tear rolling down his cheek. He walked out and dug in his saddlebags, pulled out an apple and gave it to Charlie. She brought her head up and down with her mane flowing to show her gratitude. Jim then tightened his cinch strap and climbed aboard his trusted friend and rode off in search of the sheriff's office.

Waco was not that large with a big sign denoting the office of sheriff visible from the Newton Home. Jim trotted over and got off of Charlie, wrapped his reins on the hitching post and went into the office. A large man, sitting in a chair leaning backwards against the wall, his boots crossed on the top of his desk said "Howdy Stranger, I'm John Young, the sheriff of McLennan County, What can I do for you?" He was a large man who was a quintessential western prototype. His face was rugged, with a large handlebar mustache, green eyes and a ruddy complexion. Even sitting down, he had on his gun belt with a 44 caliber revolver tied low on his hip. He appeared to be a man not to be trifled with.

"Good afternoon Sheriff", my name is Jim Walker. I served with Colonel Newton during the war. I'm heading for Runnel's county and stopped in to check on the colonel's family. Mrs. Newton said that I should check with you as there had been some Indian problems in that area."

"Yes sir, the Indians have been killing and raiding; coming down from the Llano Estacado doing their raids and getting back there before we can do anything about it."

"We have some rangers, but not enough and they are spread too thin to be effective. My deputies consist of old men and young boys who are too young or too old to go to war. And, in this day, that is young. Fourteen year old boys were dying for a lost cause, it's was just awful." the sheriff continued.

"You should be safe until you pass Brownwood, but there is a lot of Indian activity on west of Brownwood as you approach Runnels county and the settlement of Ballinger. It is my under-standing that when the Indians get too terrible, the citizens move into the deserted Fort Phantom Hill. The fort was abandoned by the Yankees at the start of the war of northern aggression. The Confederates took possession; however, they don't have enough men or arms to occupy the fort as a permanent garrison. When things get hot, the citizens move into the fort until the redskins get tired of pillaging and killing and leave or the Rangers arrive to move them out. But the Indians make it pretty difficult to live and work in the area."

"Contingents of Russian immigrants have settled Runnel's County with a continual battle between the Redskins and these newcomers. The Russians are attempting to raise wheat as a cash crop, but the Indians will come in and steal their livestock and burn their crops. Here of late, they spend more time in the fort than they do working their fields, but they refuse to give up."

Jim asked the sheriff, "Well, Sheriff Young, what do you suggest?"

The sheriff replied "Well, I would settle somewhere else, but if your mind is made up, I would be careful going through to Brownwood and then only travel at night going on to Ballinger." The sheriff asked Jim "Have you ever done any Indian fighting"

Jim answered, "Oh yes, much more than I wanted to. Due to my time in the war and fighting Redskins, I've had enough fighting to last ten lifetimes. Now I know why the land in Runnels County is so inexpensive. I'll leave out of Waco about 4:00 PM and travel all night. I'm not looking forward to this journey, but if it was easy I probably couldn't afford the land."

Jim thanked Sheriff Young and stopped by the general store again, with the same lady who had directed him to the Mrs. Nelson's home still behind the counter. She asked him if he found the home and if everything was alright. He replied it was and he was grateful for her help. He also said he needed four boxes of ammunition for his Henry repeating rifle and five boxes for his two forty-four caliber six shooters. One man with that much firepower can hold off a lot of hostiles for a long time. He got a couple of bars of stick candy and a cold soda pop, thanked the lady, mounted Charlie and headed west.

The roads west were not really roads but paths made by mounted men and a few wagons and carriages. According the lady at the store, Wells Fargo had planned a route to this part of Texas, but had to cancel it due to the war.

The travelers consisted of sojourners like Jim who really were not permanent residents and who typically, were just passing through. And it probably was not a good idea to travel directly on the road or what passed as a road. That would be where any attack would occur.

When Jim left Waco, the next settlement was Hamilton, which he should reach by daylight the following day. His plans were to find the local law enforcement agency, whether it be a sheriff or constable, make them aware of who he was and his business in their town. He would gather as much information from them as possible; especially the probability of encountering any Indians or Comancheros. He would then find a shade tree on the edge of town and bed down until almost dark.

# 31

## Homesteader Attacked by Indians

As defined previously, the moon was what was defined as a "Comanche Moon" which meant it was a full moon and almost as light as daylight. The Redskins loved a full moon so they could see to do their skullduggery. In a way Jim liked it, for he could see, but on the other hand he didn't like it because they could see him just as well. He passed several, what looked like ranch houses, which were forted up. The windows were enclosed by heavy wooden shutters with gun ports and the shutters locked from the interior.

Their livestock were enclosed in the barns and corrals which could be viewed from the house. Each house had at least two dogs which would give an alarm if unwelcome guests should come calling. Somewhere between 11:00 and 12:00 Jim saw movement ahead and pulled up under some shadows cast by a tall cottonwood tree. It appeared to be about six Indians that were visible, sneaking up on, and attempting to steal the horses in the corral from a farm house just ahead. It looked like the dogs had been killed with arrows so the alarm could not be given.

As the Indians moved silently in a group toward the pen of horses, Jim pulled his rifle out of his saddle scabbard and jumped down on the ground. He took a bead on the lead Indian and fired. He fired quickly and accurately, hitting the three men in front. The unhurt Indians fled toward their horses but were cut down by Jim's withering fire.

The farmers in the house were unsure of what to do. They opened the wooden shutters and peered out to see Jim examining the slain Redskins. Finally, a voice from the interior called out "What's going on out there?" Jim said, "My name is Jim Walker and I was just riding by when I saw these Indians stealing or trying to steal your horses."

The front door opened. The light from a kerosene lamp showed the interior of the log cabin with a man, his wife and two small children inside. The man walked out briskly and said "My name is Fritz Bauer and this is my wife Hannah. We are so grateful. We've been out here about two years with only minor trouble with the Indians."

Jim said "I hope this doesn't cause you any problems with retaliation. I think we should take them away from here and bury them, that way any other Indians will not know what happened."

It was still night, but as they learned earlier, the moon was full. Fritz harnessed the team to the wagon and the slain Indians were loaded in the back, along with picks and shovels. Fritz and Jim climbed into the wagon and drove roughly four miles into the midst of a grove of trees. It took almost until the sun was up to dig a hole big enough and deep enough to bury the dead Indians.

The loose dirt remaining after the hole was covered was shoveled into the wagon and the fresh grave was covered with leaves brushed across the fresh dirt. It would be very difficult to tell that any activity had happened there; especially the graves of six slain human beings. On the way back to Adrian's homestead the loose dirt was shoveled out of the wagon a little at a time.

When they got back to the house Mrs. Bauer had breakfast ready. They had just killed a hog and had plenty of fresh bacon and ham. It seems that killing six human beings, even Indians, would stifle one's appetite, but after what Jim had been through these past few years he was seemingly hardened to death.

Jim explained to the Bauers where he was going and why he was there when the Indians were stealing the horses. He told them he was going to Ballinger and he was traveling at night to avoid attacks from the Redskins. Mrs. Bauer spoke up and said Jim was welcome to sleep at their house until it was safe to leave that night. Mr. Bauer said "That's a really good idea. We can never repay you for what you have done for us. Maybe this will help show our appreciation."

Mrs. Bauer or Hannah, as she preferred to be called, fixed a supper for Jim that consisted of pinto beans, potatoes, corn, hominy grits and a thick crusted apple pie. He ate so much he was afraid he'd have trouble getting on Charlie. After the meal, Jim and the Bauers had an opportunity to visit. Fritz explained they had immigrated into the state in the 1850s with a large contingent of Germans at Indianola on the Texas Gulf Coast. They settled in the Hill Country around Fredericksburg. However, they had sold their homestead in the Hill Country and were lured to this area by the cheap land.

As Jim prepared to leave he told the Bauers that when he came back through he would stop and eat some more of Hannah's apple pie. The sun had just settled in the western sky when he swung into the saddle.

# 32
## Meeting with Texas Rangers

Charlie got into an easy trot and kept it up for a couple of hours. Jim came upon a stream with clear running water. He walked Charlie out into the stream and stood under the overhanging limb of a large cottonwood tree. Charlie was getting a drink when he heard voices and water splashing a little ways down from where he was. The voices were speaking the English Language. As carefully as he could, Jim called out to the distant voices. They hesitated, but they did return his greeting and ride to where he was half hidden.

The man in front, with the large brimmed hat, said his name was J. B. Walters. He further stated, "We are Rangers stationed in Austin and I was an acting jack or temporary ranger captain on a scout through what was certainly Indian Country. Jim told him who he was and of his experience back at the Bauer homestead. J. B. said he could use a good man like Jim in the rangers.

Jim told him "I am on my way to Runnels County to buy some land for a possible homestead." The Ranger said, "We are heading over to Ballinger, which was the county seat of

Runnels County. Why don't you just ride along with us for protection and get to know the boys?"

Jim told him that sounded good to him and reined his horse in with the rest of the rangers. They were not far from Hamilton where the Rangers had a safe house which consisted of two rooms, a kitchen and a long room used for sleeping quarters.

J. B. said they had been riding for two days almost non-stop; a little rest would do them some good. They would sleep for a few hours and go on to Ballinger. Buck Jackson, one of the rangers asked if they wanted him to rustle something up to eat before bedding down. J. B. told him if it was all the same to the rest of the troop, he'd rather wait until he got a few hours of sleep. Two men spent two hours shifts on guard duty and after two hours they would wake two more and the ones on prior duty would get some rest.

Jim woke to the smell of coffee and frying bacon. He looked around and saw he was the only one still in bed. Bed was defined as fully clothed lying on a cot. He quickly went out back to a cluster of oak trees and relieved himself. As he came back into the house J. B. said "There is an outhouse with paper on the west side of the house." Jim replied rather sheepishly "I just didn't know and I was in somewhat of a hurry." They had a laugh and told him to grab a plate and dig in, his breakfast was getting cold.

After breakfast, they took care of their horses and equipment. On a scout, they never took off their saddles; they simply loosened the cinches and the bits of the bridles were removed from the horse's mouth. Each horse was hobbled to allow grazing, but limit their movement. Jim had a sack of oats hung over the back of his saddle with sugar sticks tucked away in his saddle bags. J. B. formed his rangers in a squad formation and called roll. Not surprisingly, everyone was present and accounted for. They headed west toward Runnels County with J. B. and Jim in the lead.

The scout onto Ballinger was pretty uneventful except for a couple of homesteaders who had been attacked and lost some horses and other livestock. The Indians didn't like cattle because they felt they ate the grass intended for the buffalo. On the other hand, they loved horses and were excellent judges of good horseflesh. They would run the cattle out in the open pasture, kill them, take some choice cuts and let the buzzards feast on their carcasses of rotting flesh. They really did not like cattle.

As they rode into Ballinger, Jim asked J.B. "How long were they going to be in town?"

He replied "Probably a couple of days within the immediate vicinity, they had to check with the local law enforcement agencies and look into what was happening at Fort Phantom Hill." He continued, "It shouldn't take over two days. That should give you time to think over the proposition to become a ranger and check on the possibility of obtaining some farm land. We will meet you here, somewhere around six, at the courthouse two days from today."

Jim had noticed a sign posted on a building as they rode into town "Hays' Land Company." He didn't know if they sold land but if they didn't, they probably knew who was in that business. He nudged Charlie and said "Let's go and look into buying some land." He rode up to the hitching rail and dismounted. He wrapped his rein loosely around the hitching post and told Charlie "I will be back in a little while."

# 33
## Jim Becomes Land Owner

Jim walked into the office where a young lady stood behind the counter. She asked Jim if she could be of service to him. He said he hoped so; he was looking for some farm and grazing land. He continued to tell her that he was a veteran of the late war and was looking for some affordable land to settle and work.

She was about twenty years of age and stood approximately five feet tall with blonde curls that dropped almost to her waist. She was petite with a look of effortless sophistication coupled with simplicity. This was not an uncommon feature of girls who possessed good breeding and had been reared on the Texas frontier. She said "My name is Kim Burton and I just work in the office as a clerk, but I can show you some maps with the acreage pinpointed and approximate costs per acre."

She added "Mr. Sampson is the broker and has the power to finalize any deals." Kim asked Jim, "Are you looking a home to settle or just ranchland to run a herd?"

Jim told her he had lost his young wife and child in Mexia and just wanted a fresh start somewhere else with Runnels County a possibility. Kim said she was so sorry to hear about his tragedy, but they would be happy to have him as a new resident.

Jim asked "When does Mr. Sampson get into the office?" Kim looked out the front window and said, "That's him tying up to the hitching rail now. Let me introduce you two and get each of you a cup of coffee."

A tall lean man probably in his mid-forties came in the front door said hello to Kim and then directed his attention to Jim. The man was over six foot in height with lightly graying hair and a handlebar mustache. He looked more like someone who would be singing tenor in a barbershop quartet than selling land in an Indian infested territory. He spoke up and said in a clear distinctive voice "My name is Tom Sampson and I'm the broker here. Let me put my coat and bags in my office and I'll be right with you. Kim, have you got any coffee for this gentleman, Mr. uh? uh? And Kim said his name was, and she was quick to add, "You know, I don't think I even asked your name." Jim spoke up and said his name was Jim Walker from Mexia. He immediately asked,

"How much is good land selling for in Runnels County?"

Mr. Samson said "Good land is running about $10.00 an acre up to 200 acres and as you go up in size, the price per acre decreases. How much are you looking to buy, Mr. Walker? Without waiting for an answer he continued. This includes mineral, surface and subsurface water rights. Most dug wells are roughly fifteen to twenty feet deep. A stream that runs the year round is a real asset especially when running grazing livestock."

Jim said; "Let's look at properties between 100 and 200 acres and you can tell me about the Indian problems." Mr. Samson said, "We do have a Redskin problem, but they're hoping that will be remedied with the fort being re-established." Samson added, "Why do you think the land is so cheap? Well, the value of the land is directly connected to the Indian problems."

Jim and Mr. Samson spent the next two days looking at land all over the county with Jim finally deciding on a 200 acre tract with a fine creek running through it, laced with large cottonwood trees. He made his decision to buy while sitting on the shaded bank watching the birds and squirrels playing in the branches of the large trees.

Mr. Samson said, "Jim, you are one of the few Anglos buying land here. My biggest customers have been a few Mexicans and a large contingent of Russians. The Russians have bought a lot of the land and are raising wheat. They seem to be a vigorous and hardy bunch. The fierce bands of Indians did not seem to be a problem to them." Mr. Samson said, "If they lost someone to the Indians, they would still be in the fields at sunup the next morning as if nothing had happened." He added, "Another three months and they hope the Indian problem will be solved."

"I hope so, too!" replied Jim. "I expect to move here and raise a family." Samson added, "Well, the army is supposed to move back and occupy the fort, the Indians hopefully will scurry back to the Llano Estacada or Fort Sill, in the Indian Territory." And Mr. Samson added, "There is a Colonel Randall McKenzie, Commander of Fort Richardson at Jacksboro who I've heard just whipped Quanah Parker at a battle in the Palo Duro Canyon; killed their mounts and made them walk all the way back to their reservation at Fort Sill." This was similar to what happened to the Indians horses at Mexia. Jim didn't mention he was directly involved in the Indian problems in Mexia

Jim and the broker went back to the land office and made out a contract with $500.00 down and the rest financed with the remaining amount financed by Samson himself on a ten year term mortgage at 10.00% interest. The deed was executed and filed in the Runnels County Clerk's office in Ballinger. Jim was a land owner and a happy one. He just wished Laurie was there to share his excitement. He left that night for Mexia.

He again rode mostly at night. He had thought about stopping by and seeing the Bauers, but he had so much to do and so little time to do it. He was going by and meet with Mr. Spillar about starting a herd of about twenty-five heifers and two bulls. He would be willing to give back to Mr. Spillar the first calving crop and a half of the profits on his first sale of the cattle the coming year.

Jim had a pretty good nest egg from the sale of the place he and Laurie had lived on at Mexia. And, he got all his back pay when he mustered out. This was in confederate money, but he had converted into land and other tangible goods before it became completely worthless. He had to use this money to buy a team of horses and a wagon, a turning plow and leave enough cash to build some type of living quarters in the beginning. Jim was excited. And Jim was very

248

hopeful that Mr. Spillar would be agreeable to his deal or at least something he could live with.

He rode into Mexia three days later and had not encountered any problems at all. He was tired, but he was more excited than sleepy. He wanted to ride by the Pruitts and see Little Ruth and Laurie's Mom and Dad again. He still was not sure what he was going to do with Little Ruth but, he knew Runnels County was no place for a little girl with no mommy. Nevertheless, he wanted Little Ruth to remember him as a loving Daddy, not someone who came to visit from time to time.

The Pruitts were so loving and understanding to Jim and said they would keep his baby until he got on his feet.

They said they hated to see him take Little Ruth and move so far off, but they understood the difficulty in seeing things in Mexia that reminded him of Laurie everywhere he went. He didn't tell them about the proposition he was going to make to Mr. Spillar about starting the herd. He wanted to be sure Mr. Spillar agreed before he mentioned it to anyone. He ate supper with the Pruitts and reminisced about happier times. It brought tears to everyone's eyes and a heartrending ambiance. Jim finally broke the spell by standing and walking around to the Pruitts and giving each a hug. Mrs.

Pruitt said after Jim had left "That was an unusual thing for Jim to give you a hug, but that just illustrates how sweet a boy he is."

It was roughly seven O'clock on an early spring evening when he arrived at the Spillar Ranch. The sun was just beginning to hide behind the trees to the rear of the ranch house. He tied Charlie to the hitching rail, walked up on the porch and knocked on the door. The youngest of the Spillar girls opened the door; she looked at Jim and all at once started squealing, "It's Jim, its Jim, Everybody, Jim's back!" She ran up and hugged him around the waist. By this time Mr. and Mrs. Spillar and the rest of the children were rushing into the room.

Mr. Spillar said "We are all so happy to see you and that you are alright." He said to Jim, "We've already eaten, but there is plenty and I'm sure they can fix you something." Jim said "No, I had dropped by to see Little Ruth and  had eaten with the Pruitts, but thank you just the same."

Mrs. Spillar fixed some coffee and they retired to the family room. They were anxious to learn as much as possible about Jim's adventures in Runnels County. He said he had purchased two hundred acres with the opportunity to purchase more when he had the wherewithal. He told Mr.

Spillar, "I'm sure you're aware of this, but it's the little things you really don't think about that really add up in money expenses."

Mr. Spillar said he certainly understood this and he didn't want to embarrass or pry, but was he having money problems? Jim said, "Not really, but I'm trying to start a herd and that's a big investment. I've got good water, grazing land and I thought I would put about fifty acres of it into some type of feed crop for the cattle I don't have. I want to offer a business proposal to you where I would take twenty to twenty-five heifers and two bulls with the understanding that the first calving crop would be yours along with fifty percent of the profit on the sale of any cattle for the first two years.

Mr. Spillar looked taken aback by what Jim said and finally said "Jim that is too much. We consider you as part of our family. You have done a great deal for the ranch and acted so honorably as a soldier for our country. I want to offer you twenty-five head of bred heifers and two bulls to start your ranch. We will also throw in a good wagon, four plow horses and a few tools such as a turning plow, posthole diggers, harrow, hoes, a planter and shovel and anything within reason you might need to start from scratch."

251

Jim said, "I can't let you do this, that's a lot of money."

Mr. Spillar said "You're earned a lot more than what we are offering you. I just wish we could do more. You're a good man, James Jefferson Walker and it our pleasure to assist you in any way we can to get you started. We need men like you in Texas to re-build the state after this dreadful war. And, see us through all the Indian atrocities we are still experiencing."

Mr. Spillar added, "You will need drovers to herd your livestock, drive the wagon and a team of horses. They will be necessary to get the cattle drive to your new homestead in Runnels County." Also, "These cowboys probably will come in handy as they are pretty good Indian Fighters."

Jim with a look of surprise on his face said, "I really don't know what to say except thank you and I will pay you back as soon as I can."

# 34

## Jim Meets New Wife (Amanda)

Jim spent the night in the bunkhouse and got up really early, drank a cup of coffee, saddled Charlie and headed for town. His first stop was the hardware store where he was to purchase items such as staples, fence wire, etc. He was greeted by a young lady working behind the counter. She introduced herself as Amanda Hughes. She said her dad owned the store and she had just started working there as a full time employee about a month ago. She said "I have been back East for over five years at Mary Baldwin College in Staunton, Virginia." She continued, "My parents sent me off to college and the war broke out." She said "I was afraid to cross the country during the hostiles so, after she received her bachelor's degree, she continued on to get a master's degree in liberal arts. But as soon as the war was over I came home. I missed Mexia and the people here."

She asked "What about you? I don't remember you when I was growing up here as a child."

Jim took the next few minutes to bring her up to date on his history and what he was attempting to do in Runnels County.  To say the least, he was smitten with her, but he understood she was an educated southern lady who could do much better than someone like him.  The conversation went well, but again he was uncertain because he felt her station in life was substantially above his.  And, he felt that she felt that way also.

However, as he was loading up the wagon, she looked him in the eye and asked him how long he was going to be in town.  He said he really didn't know for sure, he had to purchase a wagon and team, farm implements, miscellaneous items to operate a farm/ranch and pick out roughly thirty head of livestock to be driven back to his place near Ballinger."

She said, "Good, you'll have time to take me to lunch at the buffet that just opened and the dance Friday night.  "Am I too forward?  Probably, but I've become bolder probably due to being introduced to the liberal ideas in college.  And, If you want something in life, you simply go for it.  Well, what about lunch and the dance?"

Jim was somewhat taken aback by her bravado and answered "yes" to both inquiries.  Jim asked "Do I get to pick the day or do you pick that too?"

Amanda said "Today would be nice, we never know what tomorrow will bring.  We can walk to the luncheonette from here, affording us the opportunity to get to know each other better."

He said he would be back around eleven and maybe beat the lunch-time rush. She said that sounded like a plan and she would see him then.

Jim felt like he was floating on a cloud. He couldn't believe that two educated women: Laurie and Amanda had showed some interest in him. He would always love Laurie and no one would ever take her place in his heart, but he needed someone to love and share a life with and Little Ruth needed a mother.

He rode Charlie over to the wagon yard and purchased a good, solid, used wagon and now he needed four good draft horses that were broke to pull a wagon and a plow. He would need a full complement of leather harness. He rode over to the ranch to see if Mr. Spillar had any ideas who and where to get the horses and harness. Mr. Spillar was somewhat taken aback about Jim buying a wagon when he had several he could have given him. He said "Jim, go see if you can get your money back and I'll outfit you with a good constellation wagon, a team of four draft horses, harness, plows and everything you need to get started.

Jim couldn't believe what he was hearing, He said, "You have been unbelievably good to me and I can't take anymore."

Mr. Spillar replied, "You can and you will!  You can pay me back much quicker if you have the means to get started.  I'm doing it because I want to and maybe being a little selfish thinking I can get my return on my investment quicker.  Now let's go pick out four good draft horses, harness, wagon and whatever else you might need to start the Walker Ranch.

Jim rode Charlie to town and stopped by the wagon yard and asked if he could rescind his purchase of the wagon.  The owner said "That was no problem as wagons were in short supply and they would sell quickly." He added "Because no money had changed hands, the cancellation was a simple matter."

This took a load off of Jim's mind.  He had to hurry over to the hardware store to pick up Amanda for their luncheon engagement.  Luckily, it was in walking distance from the hardware store since Jim had no transportation except for Amanda riding behind Jim on Charlie. Jim thought to himself, *she probably would have no reservations about doing that.*  Jim thought to himself, *she is a real lady who is not concerned about doing what many people might think was unladylike."* She seemed to be more concerned with getting the thing done rather than what other people might think. He smiled to himself as he guided Charlie up to the hitching rail in front of the hardware store.

Amanda was standing in front of the store with a wide smile on her face and said "It's about time Jim Walker, I've had several offers for a luncheon date in the last few minutes."

Jim quipped "Were they as handsome and wealthy as I am?"

"No, that's the reason I'm still standing here, are you ready to dine with the Queen of Limestone County?"

Jim countered by saying the queen had a choice of riding behind him on Charlie or they could walk together to the Royal Dining Hall.

She said "It would not be the first time I've ridden double on a horse, but I feel more like walking today." She said, "And, I want to introduce you to my father, Jack Hughes." They walked into the store together and she called out "Dad, I want to introduce you to someone." Mr. Hughes, who was at the rear of the store looked up, waved his hand and came to meet them.

257

Amanda said "Dad, this is Jim Walker. He has been affiliated with Mr. Spillar for roughly ten years as a ranch hand and foreman. He was a Lieutenant in the 10th Texas Regiment during the late war."

Mr. Hughes spoke up and said "I know him or at least I know who he is. He was a great benefit when the giant Indian Raid occurred and I have known the Pruitts for a long time. I know that Jim married Laurie Pruitt and they had two children with Laurie and one child dying not that long ago. The whole town was overwhelmed with grief when that occurred."

Mr. Hughes apologized for bringing forth heartrending memories and Jim cut him off "That's alright, those thoughts are continually in my mind, but I think she would like for me to go on."

Amanda jumped in and said, "Dad, I'm going to lunch with Jim, I'll be back in an hour or so. Do you think you can handle the fort while I'm gone?"

Mr. Hughes said, "I think so, go have a good time and Jim, it was good to formally meet you. And, my girl is pretty headstrong, she takes after her mother. We've been married for thirty years so it's worked out well for us."

258

"See you later, Dad" Amanda said as they strolled out the door toward the cafeteria.

The special that day was pretty much the same as every day, chicken fried steak, hash brown potatoes, gravy, salad and hot rolls.  Jim was hungry, but his mind was on Amanda, not the food before him.

Amanda asked Jim "What is your plan for the rest of your life?"

Jim excitedly told her of his plans to build the JW Ranch in Runnels County and make it the biggest and best ranch in Texas.

Jim asked "What are your plans for the rest of your life, Amanda?"

"Well, if I can speak boldly, I want to the wife of the man who builds the biggest and best ranch in Texas.  And, I want the ranch name to be the JWA Ranch with the "A" standing for Amanda.  Time is short and decisions have to be made or lost forever. I like you and I think it would a short distance to loving you. But I feel that friendship and respect is more important than what most people call love, at least in the beginning." Amanda told him.

Jim sat across the table staring at her with a piece of half eaten steak in his mouth. He finally gathered his senses and asked her "Is this a proposal of marriage?"

Amanda answered "I think it would be, in the beginning, a partnership consisting of respect and friendship with love growing over time."

"Oh, Jim I know you! Everyone in town knows you and they all love you, including my folks. I don't really feel comfortable being so bold, but this is something I want and I know I could make you a good wife and companion."

Jim said he felt honored and she would be an ideal wife for him in building the ranch. "When could you be ready to go or would she rather wait until I had a little organization on the place?"

She said "No, she wanted to be a partner from the get-go, but they really needed to get married for things to look proper."

He added, "We have to take into consideration Little Ruth, my daughter. I'm just not sure it would be prudent to take her until a shelter is built. She is currently with her grandparents and they love her so much."

Amanda told Jim, "We have to tell my parents, the Pruitts and the Spillar Family."

The rest of the week went by in a blur, they were so busy getting the wagon and filling it with all the necessary stuff. They had to pick out the heifers and bulls, select the drovers and head west early Saturday morning. This was an exciting time for Jim and Amanda as they were married on Friday Night in a simple ceremony with only the Hughes, Pruitts, Spillars and a few close friends present. Jim had absolutely no idea when he went home to Runnels County, he would be going back with a wife and all the goods necessary to start a new ranch and a new life. Everyone, including Jim, felt it was prudent to leave Little Ruth with the Pruitts until they got settled in their new home.

# 35

## The Trip to Ballinger

They were starting from the Spillar Ranch, with the cattle penned in the corral and the wagon loaded to the brim with their goods. As they were getting ready to leave, eight cowpokes, who were also part-time rangers, rode up with Mr. Spillar.

Mr. Spillar said "I am taking a little more precaution than originally thought necessary. Those beeves and draft horses would make an inviting target for those marauding Indians; I just want to protect my investment and loved ones."

Jim shook Mr. Spillar's hand and Mr. Spillar pulled Jim into a bear hug and told him how he felt about him. He hugged Amanda and told her to take care of Jim and Little Ruth when she joined them at the new ranch. The Spillars had known Amanda all her life except for the five years she had spent In Virginia. With tears in their eyes, the group said their goodbyes and Jim slapped the reins on the horse's rump and said "giddy up" and they were off to Runnels County.

Jim asked the ranger/drovers what type of formation would be best. How many drovers versus outriders would give the optimum protection?

One of the rangers spoke up and said "Jim, I think five drovers can manage the herd, with three outriders. I would suggest one outrider to the extreme right, one to the extreme left and one to the front. It would resemble a wedge." If anyone of these outriders should see anything suspicious they would ride hard for the main party, i.e., wagon and cattle. If there was imminent danger, the one seeing the danger would fire his six shooter making everyone aware that a dangerous situation was about to happen."

Jim added "That's how we used to do it in the army and what little Rangering I've done. We really need to conduct this as a ranger or military operation. We are going to go through some really hostile territory and we need to be very diligent."

The Rangers had a meeting and came back and told Jim "We have decided it would be best if you are in overall command, with our outriders rotating on a daily basis."

Jim added, "Alright, Amanda will be the wagon boss and be in charge of feeding the troops and maintaining an inventory of the water and firewood." He continued "There will be responsibilities like getting the firewood, water, etc. that we can share, no one has to do it all." Jim went on, "I've never known one of you cowboys/rangers to evade your duties, and everything will be fine." We should be there in four or five days or as they say "If the Lord is willing and the creeks don't rise."

The first day went well with no one sighting anything hostile other than a couple of rattlesnakes. It was a bright spring day with the sun shining, flowers blooming and wildlife abounding. One of those days that made you glad you're alive. The first night they encamped on the banks of a running creek which provided water for the livestock and water to wash the cooking utensils. The drovers had agreed to the number of night riders and their rotation to guard and protect the herd.

Amanda seemed to handle the wagon boss position very well indeed. She cooked supper and washed the utensils with a little help from Jim. By seven o'clock, everyone had their bedrolls laid out and the night riders were in place guarding the cattle. Amanda awoke early in the morning and started the fire for coffee and breakfast. The men, being part time rangers were used to getting up early with coffee being their most important prop-up that sustained them. Black coffee opened their eyes and kept them going well into the day. After breakfast, the men made sure their horses were fed and watered, un-hobbled and saddled for the day's work. By six o'clock, it was "Westward, Ho."

Jim and Amanda figured they would reach Waco and the Brazos River on the second day. The river could be a formable obstacle to get the cattle across. Jim said "We don't know if the river is low enough to drive them across or how many can they get on the ferry if they can't wade across." He added, "We will not know that until we get there." "We'll just have to wait and see.

# 36

## Cross the Brazos at Waco

At about four o'clock that afternoon, the city of Waco along with the winding Brazos River came into view. Jim rode out to the rangers driving the cattle and asked their advice on crossing. He knew they had been here many more times than he had on their ranger scouts. Emmitt Bailey stepped forward and said there was a really good crossing or ford just ahead. The ford was the primary reason the city was built here. Jim said, "Okay, we'll camp here for the night and cross at first light in the morning. Let's take the horses down to the river and let them drink, get some grub and get ready to cross the river at first light. We've still got a long way to go. "

The next morning they discovered the river was low enough to not only drive the cattle across, but also the wagon. This not only saved them money but also a vast amount of time. They had traveled roughly seventy to eighty miles with no mishaps. They felt very fortunate to be so lucky thus far. They left the bank of the Brazos at Waco with their next stop being the small settlement of Valley Mills, on to Hamilton and then Ballinger in

Runnels County. Their best estimate was four more days assuming no major problems.

Jim had told Amanda about the run-in with the Indians at the Bauer homestead between Hamilton and Ballinger. He added he wanted to stop by and see if they were alright. Everyone was concerned about the Indians discovering the slain comrades and tracing them back where it happened. Jim said "They're concerned about retaliation from our redskin friends."

Amanda said "That's good that you are concerned and I would like to meet them."

Jim said, "I'm not absolutely sure where it was as I came onto the property during the night and left early the next evening, but I think I would recognize it." They had come out of Hamilton after a full days travel when Jim raised his hand over his head and said "Wait a minute, I think this is it, the Bauer homestead." Jim and Amanda went to the front door and knocked. A voice from inside asked, "who's there?" Jim answered, "Its Jim Walker, the one who helped you with your Indian problem not too long ago."

"Oh Jim, it's so good to see you again! Come in, Come in. My husband, with some of our neighbors, is out checking on our livestock, the Indians have become more active lately."

Jim spoke up and said, "Mrs. Bauer, let me introduce you to my wife, Amanda."

"I didn't know you were married, Jim." Mrs. Bauer replied.

Amanda laughed and said, "He wasn't until last Friday Night."

"Congratulations, you've got a good man. He sure saved our bacon when he came through the last time."

"Thank you, he speaks very highly of both you and your husband." Amanda answered.

Jim asked, "Have you had any problems with the Indians lately?"

"No, not really, a horse stolen every once in a while is about it. They don't bother the cattle unless they are just trying to get revenge for something where they feel they have been wronged."

Jim told Mrs. Bauer, "We are moving to Runnels County to start a ranch. We've got twenty seven head of cattle, a team of horses and eight drovers/rangers to get them there. We just came by to introduce you to my wife and make sure you're alright. Tell your husband hello and if you're near Ballinger, come to see us."

# 37

## Jim Meets Lone Eagle

Jim and Amanda climbed back on the wagon and slapped the horses' rumps with the reins and started in a slow trot to catch up with the drovers and the cattle. The drive was pretty uneventful until just before they got into Runnels County when about twenty-five to thirty Indians showed up and rode on the southern side of the herd. The outriders had seen them and warned Jim and the rest of the party. Jim brought the herd in close to the wagon and everyone was issued a Winchester Repeating Rife and lots of ammunition.

One Indian with a headdress, presumably a chief, rode in and asked one of the rangers for a parley. The ranger rode back to convey this request to Jim. Jim asked the ranger "What do you think?"

The ranger said "I don't know, but I personally would parley." He said "They could take what they wanted from us with loss. Why not talk to them, we can always fight."

The Indian Chief said his name was Lone Eagle and he was a Comanche, one of Quanah Parker's

Band but they were not with Quanah at the Palo Duro Fight.

He said, "We had slipped away the night before and were attempting to make it to Mexico." He continued, "We are hungry, the buffalo are gone and we have not been able to provide enough by hunting. We have some guns, but little ammunition." He continued "If you could help us we would be forever grateful, forever."

Jim could see the sincerity in his eyes and feel the hunger in his voice. He asked the chief, "What do you need?"

He answered, "I have fifty braves who have not eaten for three or four days. We need some of your beeves for food."

Jim asked him, "How many do you need?"

The chief said "We need ten head of cattle to keep going."

Jim said "I can give you five, but if I gave you more than that I would not have enough to start up my ranch in Runnels County." Jim continued by saying that he would have to fight if he insisted on ten head.

Lone Wolf looked sad, but submissive; he said "Alright, we will make every attempt to make five cattle do.

The drovers cut out five heifers and the Indians drove them off as they left the area. Jim said to Amanda, "This will cut down our herd but it probably saved our lives. And, I'll bet we haven't heard the last of Chief Lone Wolf."

Amanda laughed and said his name was Lone Eagle. He grinned and told her he was a little nervous. It was not the last they had heard of Lone Eagle. In the coming years, when the chief made his trips from the Llano Estacada in far West Texas to Mexico, he would always stop by the ranch and spend a day of two. The Walkers would always have a big celebration with a barbecue. Each visit, Jim would allow the Chief and his braves to take five head of cattle as a remembrance of their first meeting on the trail to Runnels County.

He then asked Amanda if she could drive the wagon on to Ballinger while he went on ahead to make arrangements for their arrival. He needed to buy some fence posts since these cattle needed to be penned in a corral until a larger pasture was fenced.

Jim said, "I also need to see the land man about the Indian problem that was supposedly being solved when I was last here."

Amanda said "I'll only be an hour or so behind you, I'll be alright. And, I'll have eight young Texas Rangers to keep me company while you're gone, she said with a grin."

"Alright, alright," Jim replied, I'll hurry!"

When Jim got to Ballinger, he went directly to the Samson Land Company where he found Kim, still sitting behind the counter. Jim asked for Mr. Samson, but Kim said he would not be back until early afternoon.

"Could I help?" she asked.

Jim replied, "Well, the JWA Cattle Company was about to arrive with twenty heifers, two bulls, four draft horses, a wagon loaded with equipment and eight Texas Rangers acting as drovers. I need to buy some fence posts and wire."

Kim said "They have just invented something they call "Barbed Wire" and it works wonderfully. We have a lumber company here in town where you will be able to buy posts, but you'll have to buy your fencing wire at the hardware store." She continued, "I think there is enough open range where you can cut some cedar posts and there may be enough on your place."

Jim added, "Also, I lost part of my herd to Indians by using them as a bargaining tool to save our lives. Your boss had assured me the Indians menace was pretty much over."

They both looked out the window at the same time and saw the cattle kicking up dust as the wagon and the livestock entered the town square. Jim said, "Kim, you are now looking at the whole of JWA Cattle Company accompanied by eight (8) Texas Rangers. Oh, and that beautiful lady driving the wagon is my new wife, Amanda."

Jim went over to the wagon and told Amanda that he had to go by the lumber company to check on fence posts and to the hardware store to check on fencing wire.

She said "Climb on board and tell me where to go." He said "I'm not absolutely sure, but I think the lumber company is on the second block off of the square and the hardware store about two blocks north of the lumber company. Let go and see if we can find them."

Jim told the rangers to "just hold the cattle on the square until they could drive them to his place." He had to do some business in town before they went out to the ranch.    He then went to the lumber company and the hardware store and purchased enough posts for the corral and enough wire for the corral and the big pasture.  As it was getting on toward night, they decided to night camp their cattle and hobble their horses.

They went back to the town square and picked up the rangers and their cattle.  He hoped he could find the future home of the JWA Cattle Company.  He remembered it was more or less five miles north of town with a large creek and a clump of giant oak and cottonwood trees where he had thought the main house and headquarters would be, subject to Amanda's approval.

# 38

## Their New Home

Mr. Samson had put markers on each corner of the property to denote boundaries. Jim had a metes and bounds legal description in his bags. When they came over the last rise, the sun was just going down behind the giant oak trees, it looked like a masterpiece painted by an artist. Jim reached over and squeezed Amanda's hand and said "Well, there is where I thought the headquarters for the JWA should be, right among those oak trees. What do you think? Do you like it?"

Amanda exclaimed, "Oh! Jim, it's absolutely beautiful!"

Jim replied "It is beautiful, almost as beautiful as you, but nothing is as beautiful as you."

Jim pulled her close to him, looked into her eyes and whispered "thank you for being here and sharing this moment with me, I will treasure it forever."

Jim continued, after some pause and said "Amanda, I never thought I could have feelings for another woman after Laurie. She was my life and the mother of my children. Don't be jealous of my feelings for her as she would not be jealous of you. I'm not sure if the roles were reversed I would not be jealous of her having feelings for another man, but I'm sure she would not. I'm only sure of one thing; that I'm the luckiest person in the whole wide world and I love you with all my heart."

"Now, let's unload the wagon and get the show on the road. Probably, the first thing we need to do is feed this hungry bunch of drovers. There is something I've been pondering since we've started on this trip, should we change the name JW Cattle Company to JAW or even AJW Company?" Amanda laughed and said "No, just leave it the way it is, you started it and got it going and I want to see if it is successful before I lend initials to it." They both laughed and went to work unloading the wagon.

Jim and Amanda had not had much privacy during their marriage and it didn't look as if that would change anytime in the near future. The headquarters for the JWA Cattle Company was a bare prairie with oak and cottonwood trees and a running creek. That was fine for old married folks, but for newlyweds it was not so good. There were not any hotels or any other places of privacy that they were aware of.

The next three weeks were spent in frenzy. The Rangers/Cowboys spent the time building a log cabin with a cellar underneath with a staircase and a trap door. The house was a long house with two bedrooms on one end and a kitchen and dining/family room on the other. Each end had a pot bellied wood burning stove to provide heat. They had found good water when they struck an artesian aquifer at about twenty feet below the surface.

The corral was built with *a lean-to* shelter to protect the livestock with enough storage for the livestock feed. The last week was spent with all hands including Jim and sometimes Amanda, building the fence around the perimeter of the two hundred acres and a cross fence to protect the cultivated region. At the end of three weeks, Jim and Amanda cooked a really big meal and had a thank you celebration for the Rangers. Jim gave each of them $10.00, which was a month's pay for a Ranger. He also wrote a sincere letter of gratitude to Mr. and Mrs. Spillar and his promise to repay them for their generosity and kindness. He told the Rangers they always had a place to stay anytime they were on a scout out their way. And he added "Be careful, there are still hostiles out there." When the Rangers rode off back to Mexia, Jim and Amanda were lost in happiness as things had gone better than they ever could have imagined.

And, they were going to be alone for the first time since they married on what seemed like a long ago Friday night.

At the end of the first year, there were a full crop of calves and a new member of the Walker family and Little Ruth had come to live as a member of the family again. Amanda and Jim had made a trip back to Mexia to get some supplies, see relatives and pick-up their precious package of Little Ruth. The Pruitts knew this day would come but it was still a sad occasion for them and for Little Ruth too. She had come to look upon the Pruitts as her mother and father. At the time, Amanda was pregnant with their first child. Jim jokingly said he hoped it would be a boy because he needed some man help around the JAW Cattle Company.

Well, it was a girl, but after he looked into her big blue eyes he said with a wide grin "I can handle the workload for a while longer." Amanda declared that she wanted to name the little girl, Addie Bernice. Jim said that it sounded like a beautiful name and Addie Bernice it would be.

Amanda said to Jim, "Jim, I've got a secret that I think you should know."

Jim said with a chuckle "I think this is the time to get all these secrets out in the open." He looked at Amanda and said "Well, out with it."

Amanda bowed her head and sheepishly said, "My name is not Amanda or that's only part of it."

"Wow, that is a deep dark secret, tell me everything, girl." She said "my name is Barbara Amanda Victoria Hughes Walker." Jim brought her into his arms and said "That is a beautiful name for a gorgeous woman."

The following year was a frenzy of activity with much accomplished but never enough. There was so much to do and never enough time. But it was fun. They were well on their way to repaying the Spillars and they had acquired more acres of land and transferred it from raw prairie into well manicured, plowed farm land. There was only one fly in the ointment; the Indians were still a nuisance.

# 39

## A Killing Raid (Indians)

One morning Amanda was on the back porch and she saw several riders sauntering across the prairie; roughly, she guessed, a good mile distance. They were heading for their ranch but not in a big hurry. Little Ruth, along with two neighbor girls, were playing in the back yard and the new baby, Addie Bernice, was asleep in the bedroom. Jim was with the neighbor girl's father, Philip Hobson and they were out checking on their cattle. It appeared that someone had cut their fences the night before, allowing their cattle to get out of their pastures.

After following the cattle and some unshod pony tracks for a long and exhausting distance, the cattle were found. Several of the cows were dead with spears in their bodies. Philip said "Why would they do that, they are no good to them dead." Jim said "Because they don't like cattle and to draw us away from our unprotected places with our women and children there."

"Oh Lord" Philip exclaimed, "My poor wife and children."

"These are Redskins out on a killing raid." Jim said with tears in his eyes "I'm afraid you're right. You go to your house and I'll go to mine. If your family is alright come on to my house and I'll do the same.

Amanda with urgency, screamed at Nancy, "Grab the girls and get into the underground room." I've already put Addie down there in her basket, luckily she is asleep. Instruct the girls to be quiet as a mouse, these are bad people."

Before she left the upstairs, she grabbed four Winchester Repeating Rifles and four boxes of ammunition. She almost fell as she was going down the stairs to the cellar beneath the ranch house. Mrs. Hobson was a crack shot as was Little Ruth. She was assuming the Hobson girl knew how to handle a rifle. It was mandatory that the women and children were well trained in firearms and horsemanship.

Amanda handed the rifles to each of the girls and Mrs. Hobson. She had left the front door open and the window shades up so she could see what they were doing outside of the house. She ran back up the stairs and grabbed another repeater and four more boxes of shells. She was preparing for a long siege and she was really concerned for Jim and Philip.

When she looked out the window, she noticed they had stopped at the barn and were looking in her direction. She hurriedly left the trap door about half way up and stood on the stairs so she could see their movement. About ten of the Bucks from the larger group rode up to the house and stopped at the edge of the open porch. She could see them, but they couldn't see her. She was very concerned that the baby would wake up and start crying, revealing their presence in the house. After what seemed like a lifetime, probably no more than ten minutes, they rode off and joined the larger group at the barn.

They were probably trying to decide their strategy. They were going to attack, it was just a matter of where, when and how. Just then several rifle shots were heard, Amanda pushed up the door and saw Jim riding hard toward the house. The Indians were surprised and did not react in time to put a stop to him reaching the house. He jumped off his mount and raced for the open front door. It was fortunate Amanda had left it open.

With the Jim there, the strategy changed completely. The Walkers had six rifles with a stockpile of ammunition. However, one of these rifles was left in the saddle scabbard when Jim jumped off of his horse onto the porch. Still, this

282

should be enough firepower. They needed someone to watch all sides of the house and direct their fire in the direction most needed. After about half an hour, a long rider was seen riding like the wind toward the house. It was Philip coming from the Hobson Place to join in the fight. He didn't know for sure where his family was at this time. He rode hard to the porch and with rifle in hand clambered into the front door. Philip was overjoyed to find his family with the Walkers, safe.

Jim greeted Philip and was really glad to see him safe and sound. Jim said "I think our best strategy would be to shoot their horses, they are easier to hit and will thwart an attack" Comanche Indians are the best light cavalry in the world when mounted, but they are not as terrifying on foot. So, aim for the horse, we've got to keep them at a distance so they can't get close enough to set the house on fire." The girls were old enough to reload the rifles and have one at ready when the shooters ran out of ammunition.

Philip said, "I can hit what looks like the chief with that feathered headdress."

Jim said "no, let's make them start the ruckus." Jim continued, "Maybe, they will just go away, not likely, but maybe"

283

Jim said to Amanda where did she put those field glasses? Amanda replied, she thought they were in the cedar chest. "I'll get them for you." Sure enough, the glasses were there and she handed them to Jim. Jim looked with interest for probably ten minutes and directed his attention to Philip "There seems to be an animated discussion or argument between what appears to be the chief and the younger braves and it appears the chief is losing."

Philip asked the question that everyone had on their mind, "Can they win this fight?" Jim, who had been in many skirmishes or firefights said with some degree of resignation in his voice, "They certainly have the numbers on their side, but the cost of victory would be high." Jim continued, "The odds are certainly on their side, but that is not to say they can't pull it off." Jim said "I would imagine that was what the argument was all about." "The old Chief probably wants to go find easier pickings."

They were trying to joke to mask their fear. They were in a world of hurt and they needed help but they had no idea where that help would come from. Jim and Philip had decided about four o'clock that if the Indians did not attack by five o'clock, they would fire upon the Indians at the barn if they were still there. They wanted it over by dark, one way or the other.

About four thirty, the Indians lined up their ponies facing the front of the ranch house for what appeared to be a frontal attack. Jim alerted everyone to get into position and check their weapons and be ready. One of the younger braves was directing the attack and they came riding hard toward the ranch house.

Jim told them "to hold your fire until I give you the order to commence firing and remember, shoot the horses. Also, have your targets picked out before you fire. When you run out of shells, the girls should have another rifle loaded and ready for you." When the first wave was roughly fifty feet away, the order was given to fire. The Indians melted away like wheat cut by a sickle under the scalding fire. Another wave was ordered forward with the same results. Not many Indians were casualties, but they were afoot.

The attacks stopped for a time while the young braves seemingly were again clambering for another frontal attack. Jim estimated they had time for one more assault before darkness set in. He had heard that Indians did not like to fight at night. He didn't know if there was any truth to that or if it was an old wives tale. He certainly hoped they would wait until daylight to continue their fight.

As nighttime fell, the Indians built large campfires near the barn and the corral. With the brightness of the large fires you could see their activities from the house, but what was important was they did not create any hostile activities toward those in the ranch house. The night was spent trying to devise a better strategy for the defense, come daylight. The Indians evidently were not going anywhere and it seemed like they were willing to pay the price for the victory, whatever it might be. Those in the house slept in shifts with sleep hard to come by.

# 40

## The Arrival of Lone Eagle

When the first rays of daylight came streaking across the night sky, everyone knew the breaking of day was close at hand. As the sun started rising over the trees in the east, they saw a hazy line of what appeared to be horses, with riders stretching across the horizon as far as the eye could see. The Indians had received reinforcements during the night and now it seemed even more hopeless than before.

The new Indians were probably more than a mile away and they didn't appear to be joining up with the hostiles at the barn. Philip and Jim were discussing how to best defend their homestead when a small party from the new arrivals came riding straight for the house. They really didn't know what to make of the situation, but they were scared. There appeared to be a chief in the group, based on his feathered head dress.

They didn't veer off and go to the group at the barn but kept coming straight for the house. If they had gone to the other Indians Jim would have been really concerned, but now he was just scared and confused. When they got within fifty yards in the dim light he thought he recognized his old friend, Chief Lone Eagle. As they drew closer, it was possible to determine that it was him.

With his arm raised over his head indicating a sign of peace, he rode up to the porch and dismounted. He came through the front door and made the universal peace sign and said "Good Friend, Jim Walker, we've come to help. A group of renegade Apache, Kiowa and Comanches have left the Reservation at Fort Sill on a murder raid. A chief's son was killed by a drunken white man over in Big Springs and he is seeking revenge. He is the one at the barn with the headdress on."

Lone Eagle continued "I'm going down and talk reason to him and if that does not work, we will fight him. Jim Walker is my friend."

Jim said to Lone Eagle, "We are so grateful and we will go with you to talk to the chief."

Lone Eagle replied, "No, he is an old friend who has let his grief control him. For his sake and the sake of his tribe he must go back to the reservation and take his young braves with him. I have enough braves to win but at what cost?" Stay inside the house and close all your windows and doors until this is over. It should not take long for this to be settled."

The chief briskly walked out the door and mounted his horse. He rode slowly down to the barn and raised his hand in greeting to his old comrade. They moved away from the large group and talked, just the two of them. Every once in a while, a young buck would wander over and make some animated arm and hand gestures, but it appeared he was rebuked by the old chief.

After a period of time, the two chiefs stood facing each other and placed a hand on the shoulder of the other. They had come to an agreement that was acceptable to them both. The chief went over to his group of braves at the barn while Lone Eagle mounted his horse and started riding back to the ranch house. He dismounted at the porch, tied his horse to the railing and came in the front door. He told Jim he had promised the other chief they would give him twenty head of cattle to feed his Indians, was that OK? Jim remarked, "That is better than our scalps and all of our cattle." Mr. Hobson said he would furnish half of the cattle they wanted. Jim added, "We also will give some beeves to Lone Eagle and his braves."

Jim told Lone Eagle "If you could stay around for awhile I am sure I could get the other ranchers in the area to contribute some cattle. Lone Eagle, you and your braves could drive the livestock up

289

across the Red River and start a ranch. I've heard that's what Quanah Parker did after he went in and everyone has said he's been quite successful."

The next week was spent riding from ranch to ranch explaining the plan of supplying Lone Eagle and his band with seed cattle to start ranching activities in the Indian Territory. He knew Burk Burnett and Waggoner and other big ranchers had advised and assisted Quanah Parker in becoming successful. As the ranchers said, it was simply an investment to protect their own herds. The Indians were going from cattle rustlers to cattle raisers.

As they watched him ride off with his entourage of Braves, there was a bit of sadness in their hearts as they realized that a way of life was ending.

Since their discovery of the horse that was brought to Texas by the Spanish conquistadors, the Indians became almost impossible to defeat. As previously stated, they were known as the best light Calvary in the world.

The White Man entered Texas in the early 1820s with the Indians unconquerable until the Battle of Palo Duro Canyon in the 1870s. The Indians were only beaten then because they were separated from their horse herd. This was a half century of the Indian reigning supreme. It is the longest war the country had ever fought.

# Epilogue
## Jim Reflects on His Life

The next few years went by quickly, the Walker family had moved into a new, larger, rock and plank house supplied with inside water from a windmill. Jim had repaid Mr. Spillar in monetary terms, but he could never repay him for everything he had done. He had acquired over twenty-five thousand acres of land through purchase or a binding option to purchase. He also had roughly 5,000 head of San Gertrudis Cattle, a new breed of cattle developed in South Texas on the King Ranch. Life was good and they had been lucky. But it was the result of hard work of both Amanda and him, a labor of love. Jim and Amanda's philosophy was that everyone needed some luck, but they felt that the harder you worked, the luckier you got.

Amanda and Jim had five additional children, three boys and two girls with Little Ruth being the sixth and oldest. Of course, Little Ruth was the child of Laurie and Jim. And, to Amanda's undying credit, she never let Little Ruth forget who her real mother was or what a wonderful person she was and how she had loved her.

Amanda home schooled all the children with Little Ruth going on to pass her college entrance exam at Baylor University and later her entrance exam to obtain her law degree from Baylor in Waco. She had a law office in Waco and had served two terms as a state representative from their District. She handled all the legal matters of the ranch, which filled most of her time. She was still a single lady. She said she just hadn't had the time to marry up with anyone yet, but she said she would evidently."

Three of her brothers and sisters had spent four glorious years at Texas A&M with the youngest member of the family being a Junior, enrolled at the University of Texas at Austin. Jim and Amanda were very proud of their children and rightfully so.

They had suffered the hardships and privations of early childhood and had become hard working, responsibility young adults. They were a credit to themselves and their community. The older ones experienced the hardships that a "new country" necessitates. It put more stiffness in their backbone and enabled them to meet life's challenges. Jim had been approached many times to run for Congress and Governor of the state, but he felt he could be more beneficial belonging to and helping to guide organizations like the

Southwestern Cattlemen's Association, Quarter Horse Association and other local grass roots organizations. He also loved to cross breed cattle, always shooting for a better, fatter and hardier breed of livestock.

Jim never felt special. He had been favored by having special friends such as the Spillars, his surrogates parents (the Pruitts) and two of the most beautiful and gracious wives in the world. His main regret in life was Bobby. He never got over losing Bobby at Franklin. And, that he never retrieved his body and took it home before Bobby's Mother and Dad passed. He continually carried the burden of convincing a reluctant Bobby into going back into the 10th Texas before that last battle at Franklin. He went back to West Columbia to visit the cemetery every five years on the anniversary of the battle. It always made him melancholy, but it was something he felt he owed his friend. He would sometimes wonder why a good person like Bobby's life was cut short and he had such a full and wonderful one.

He also regretted the inability of sharing his children with their grandparents in Mississippi. Due to the war and distance, they were shut out of their lives. This was something both James and Amanda reflected on frequently.

James did love life and much of that adoration of life was Jim's love of being a rancher. He loved to sit on the front porch of their ranch house and remember those long ago days, when riders in the distance were spotted and you didn't know if it was Lone Eagle or a hostile band arriving for mischief. Jim was happy with his life and his family. God is good, all the time!

# The End

Printed in Great Britain
by Amazon.co.uk, Ltd.,
Marston Gate.